HEY MOM

STORIES FOR MY MOTHER, BUT YOU CAN READ THEM TOO

LOUIE ANDERSON

with

ANDREW POSTMAN

TOUCHSTONE

NEW YORK   LONDON   TORONTO   SYDNEY   NEW DELHI

Touchstone
An Imprint of Simon & Schuster, Inc.
1230 Avenue of the Americas
New York, NY 10020

First Touchstone hardcover edition April 2018

TOUCHSTONE and colophon are registered trademarks
of Simon & Schuster, Inc.

For information about special discounts for bulk purchases,
please contact Simon & Schuster Special Sales at 1-866-506-1949
or business@simonandschuster.com.

The Simon & Schuster Speakers Bureau can bring authors to your live event. For
more information or to book an event, contact the Simon & Schuster Speakers
Bureau at 866-248-3049 or visit our website at www.simonspeakers.com.

Interior design by Kyle Kabel

Manufactured in the United States of America

10   9   8   7   6   5   4   3   2   1

Library of Congress Cataloging-in-Publication Data

Names: Anderson, Louie, author.
Title: Hey mom : stories for my mother, but you can read them too / by
    Louie Anderson.
Description: New York : Touchstone, [2018]
Identifiers: LCCN 2017059109 | ISBN 9781501189173 (hardcover) |
    ISBN 9781501196379 (hardcover [signed])
Subjects: LCSH: Anderson, Louie. | Anderson, Louie—Family. | Mothers—
    United States. | Mother and child—United States. | Comedians—Family
    relationships—United States.
Classification: LCC HQ759 .A4935 2018 | DDC 306.874/3—dc23 LC record
available at https://lccn.loc.gov/2017059109

ISBN 978-1-5011-8917-3
ISBN 978-1-5011-8919-7 (ebook)

To all moms

Ora Zella Anderson

I'm your mother. Do you know what that means?
Does it mean anything to you?

—Christine Baskets

CONTENTS

CONTENTS

— 2016 —

CONTENTS

— 2017 —

CONTENTS

The first words out of my mom's mouth at a restaurant: "Could we get some extra butter, please?"

Maître d': "Well, let us seat your party first, ma'am."

—

My mom will go to any garage sale. She'll stop no matter what.

"Pull over, Louie, that looks like a good sale."

"So we're leaving the funeral procession?"

"Well, he's not going anywhere."

If my mom could come back from the beyond, I'm pretty sure she would stop at a garage sale before she came to see me.

—

My mom was the sweetest person in the world but she was a thief. You always knew what she was going to steal. At a restaurant, she'd point out the item she was going to take. She'd say, "Louie, aren't these cute salt-and-pepper shakers?"

"I'll see them when I get home."

Then my brother got caught shoplifting. My mom said, "Where'd he get an idea like that?"

"I don't know, Mom, should we look at the salt-and-pepper wall? You're one shaker from a felony."

—

She drove in the imaginary lane.

"What are we doing over here, Mom?"

"Well, no one's in it."

"You're the worst driver in the world."

"I've never had an accident."

"Yeah, but how many have you caused?"

—

We had eleven kids in our family. I was tenth of eleven. I just slid out. I was home from the hospital before she was. I was waiting at the door. "I'm starving!"

— APRIL 2015 —

It's About Time

Hey Mom!

I already talk about you a lot but lately I've been speaking to you directly, too, so I figured it was time I wrote. I often wonder how you're doing. Is there an afterlife? Heaven? That's the million-dollar question. Or billion-dollar question. Or in this day and age, I guess the trillion-dollar question. A million's not even a million anymore. A million was really a million back in your day, Mom.

I could say I'm writing now to tell you about this great role I got in a great TV show, which just got "picked up," in which I play a mom—that's right, Mom, a *mom*, not a dad—of four grown sons, and the character is so much like you! Her name is Christine Baskets and playing her comes so naturally because I keep channeling you. *What would Mom say? What would Mom do? What would Ora Zella Anderson do?*

So of course I want to let the inspiration for the character know about it, even if she died a quarter-century ago.

But that's not the only reason I feel the need to write. I have so many questions and so many things I've been meaning to say to you. Stuff that's on my mind a lot, and I wanted to get it down someplace. There were questions I neglected to ask Dad when he was still around but that's easier to explain. There were so many things he wouldn't talk about. He was angry, an angry alcoholic.

Sometimes I just didn't want to be around him, and neither did any of your other ten children.

But why didn't I ask *you* the things I want to ask you now, back when I had the chance? You had no trouble talking, Mom. "Blah, blah, blah," Dad said many times about your "going on." I'm so much more like you than him, in that way. You never yelled or punished or expressed disappointment, only love. Sometimes I wish you'd been harder, more disapproving. Maybe you were and I didn't notice. Anyway, it kills me that I didn't ask you a bunch of things I think about more and more these days.

I often think about childhood and our family and the things that make us who we are. I've always thought about that stuff. You know this, Mom, but so much of my comedy act over the years has been based on our family, and you, and what growing up was like. That was a lot of my best material, still is. As a young comic, I mostly made fat jokes at my own expense, or maybe I should say I did lots of fat jokes about this fat character I played onstage (though I played a fat person offstage, too). That was the common denominator. But it's come to be less of my act. Maybe it's because I don't see myself anymore as a fat person but a person who happens to be fat.

Anyway, you were still around when I was doing material about family and it always got laughs, but then I got a little darker and maybe more real with it, and got some of the biggest laughs of the set. A different kind of laugh. It opened up something in me and I started digging. Roman DiCaire, an older comedian I admired and who saw me perform, told me, "Louie, if you do that material about your family and have a completely clean act, you'll be famous." I lacked direction then and I was looking for someone to tell me something. He turned out to be 100 percent right. Decades later,

4

Mom, I make jokes about the family, and they land, and land hard, because they're so true for everyone, though I still think our family was way more screwed up than most. "A stress test—you know what that is? It's where you have your whole family over to the house." Stuff like that often gets the most unguarded laugh of the night.

So here I am, Mom, on the verge of basically playing you for a national TV audience, with the pursed lips, the disapproving judgmental glances—in the nicest way—that I picked up from you. You know that side glance that could say a million things—*Don't do that, Put that down, What are you doing? Don't make us look bad, Oh, Louie . . .* ? That's there.

Yet even though I understand some things about you and me, I want to understand more.

Which brings me to tonight, Sunday night, this hotel suite desk, in Room 117—eleven and seven, two good numbers if you're from Las Vegas, Mom, which is where I now live—of the Hilton Garden Inn in Erie, Pennsylvania, having just come from finishing my sixth show in four days (one show Thursday night, two each Friday and Saturday nights, and tonight's), my fifty-eighth comedy set of the year. I'm writing to tell you about how it's going, and keeping you even more alive with me. I have so much to report, about so many things, some good stuff, some not so good. But it's a lot, and who knows, maybe one day it will all turn into a book. If it does, I know what I want to call it: *Hey Mom*, because so many times since you've been gone I've looked up and said out loud, "Hey Mom, what do you think of this?"

"Hey Mom, get a load of this guy!"

"Hey Mom, how'd I get into this mess?"

"Hey Mom, what am I doing with my life?"

I think we all do a subconscious "Hey Mom" a lot of the time.

I guess I must believe in the afterlife if I'm writing to you and I talk to you and my face is always turned up to the sky. If there *is* an afterlife, I hope there's a big comfortable chair, because I know you like that, and good creamer for your coffee, and a TV showing old reruns.

The last time I had a moment like this, where I absolutely needed to write down what was on my mind, was 1987, when I was touring the Midwest and doing Summerfest in Milwaukee. Thousands and thousands of people were taking in the different acts, drinking beer, eating bratwurst. When my set was over, I wanted to head back to the hotel, so I got a lift from a festival volunteer. I climbed into the back seat of the car—a Buick. Mom, you always loved Buicks, such big beautiful cars. All around us were so many drunks wobbling and staggering to their cars, then getting into their cars and trying to avoid hitting other drunks. My first thought was amazement at the inner gyroscope of drunks, how the alcohol takes over and they look like they're going to fall over but somehow they don't—amazing! A lot of them, mostly men, made wrestling noises. *Ooo! OOOOO!*

But I had a bigger thought: The whole scene was a metaphor for my life, me swerving and trying to avoid the damage that alcohol did to me, did to all of us, does to all kinds of people. That it did to you, Mom, though you yourself hated to drink. As soon as I got to my room at the Pfister Hotel, a beautiful old hotel in Milwaukee that's supposedly haunted, I sat down at the desk, just like I'm doing here with you, and I wrote a letter to Dad. He was already seven years dead at that point, and it all just spilled out of me, letter after letter in my journal, and I kept writing, and crying, in search of some better understanding, any understanding, for why Louis William Anderson was such a cruel, difficult alcoholic father. Those letters eventually got collected into a book, *Dear Dad: Letters from an Adult Child,* that you got to see, Mom, but just barely, because you died without warning a few months later.

Like I said, so much has happened since then, and I want to keep you up-to-date. I wish you had seen the professional success I've enjoyed in the twenty-five years since you died. You deserve a lot of the credit, partly because I talk so much about you and the family in my act, partly because of the reservoir of love and kindness you doled out to me and to all of us, which gave me the strength to not quit. Because you never quit, never gave up, never gave in, always put one foot in front of the other. In a couple years it will be forty years for me as a stand-up comic. A clown, really, but a clown who's making good money. Can you believe that, Mom? Forty! Anyway, I could not have gotten this far in my career if I gave up easily. Dad was also stubborn. All us Andersons are. We won't give in, we won't give up, we won't even take care of ourselves.

There are other things I wish. I wish I would have had you come live with me later in life. I wish I'd been more open to the idea. I know you would have adored that. I would have, too, eventually. I was selfish then, much more than I think—I hope—I am now. I wish I would have done it and I'm glad to say it here even though it's too late. I also know we have to let go of regrets or it drags us through the mud for all the things we didn't do.

I need to tell you about the family—but it's late and I'm wiped out from the show, so I'll say good night for now. I'll write tomorrow.

Love,
Louie

Gone But Never Forgotten

Hey Mom,

So there are five Anderson kids left, Mom, which I'm really sorry to say means that six of us have passed away since you left us. Or maybe you know that. Are things getting more complete up there, wherever you are, as each of your children joins you? Or does each one make you sadder, because they've left us, here? That's how you were, Mom—you would have thought of us, not yourself. Will it only be complete when we're all up there? I hope there's no fighting there. I hope there's enough butter. I hope there's enough love. "Enough love"—there's a strange idea. A mistaken idea. Love's a constant. That's a hard lesson to learn.

And—here's a small thing—do I even believe that stuff about the afterlife and heaven? Or is it just that I want to?

Those of us still here—Jimmy, Shanna, Lisa, little Tommy, and me—are very close. We don't see each other as much as we should but we're close. I live in Las Vegas, Mom—I know you always liked Vegas, the buffets, the big hotels, the free giveaways, coming to town with two suitcases, one of them empty, and leaving with both full—and my remaining two sisters and two brothers live in the Midwest: Minnesota, Wisconsin, South Dakota. I visit Minnesota ten or twelve times a year. Altogether, there are more than fifty Anderson nephews and nieces, great-nephews and nieces, and great-great-nephews and nieces. I really should get an exact count. A lot of them have escaped the family curse, fortunately, but DNA runs deep, and more than a few have been through drug abuse and other addictions.

Can you believe it's 2015, Mom? That used to sound like a year from science fiction. *"2015 and beyond . . ."* But here we are. Can you believe I'm still alive, considering all the crap I've done, the risks I've taken, the lifestyle I've lived? Things are really different now. You would be so thrilled and also so damn disappointed, especially with how people treat each other.

Am I jumping around too much in my letters? It's no different from how we used to talk, you and me. The mind wanders when it's never totally satisfied. But I guess that's kind of self-evident, right?

At some point, I'll write to you about the day you died, though I don't know if you even want to hear it. But I will get to it. I'm finding new reservoirs of strength. I really love you and miss you and wish I would have been nicer to you. Did I say that yesterday? Does everyone say they wish they were nicer to their mom or dad after it's too late? I hope everyone remembers to call their mom and dad and say "I love you" because you never know. When I would call and do that with Dad, he wouldn't respond to me, he would just yell at you, "What the hell's wrong?! He's saying he loves me and he loves you! Get on the phone and find out if he's in jail!"

Everyone should tell the people they love that they love them, at all times, because you never know. You always said that, Mom: "You never know." I wish you were alive right now, no matter how old you'd be. I just turned fifty, twelve years ago! No, I don't like saying my age. I got your vain streak. I wish I would have got more of your nice streak because you were the nicest person I ever met or knew. I got more of Dad's mean streak than I'd like, his sneer and judgmental way, though I've worked on that a lot. ("I hate that guy!" he'd say. "But you don't even know the guy," I'd say. "I don't have to know him to hate him!" he'd say.) I was going to say I also got Dad's addictive personality but maybe it was yours, too, Mom, because I know you loved food. I've had trouble with drinking, drugs, gambling, and especially food. I survived the drugs, gambling, and drinking. I quit smoking fifteen years ago. But I'm still working on the food.

Oh yeah: I'm addicted to laughs and applause, too. I love them. No calories yet very filling! The better the show, the less I eat afterward. True.

I'm looking forward to playing you more on TV. It'll be a treat and I know you'd get a big kick out of it. I'll try to write again tomorrow.

Night, Mom.

Love,

Louie

P.S. Say hi to Kent, Rhea, Roger, Mary, Sheila, and Billy. Say hi to Dad, if he's there. I hope there's no drinking up there, Mom.

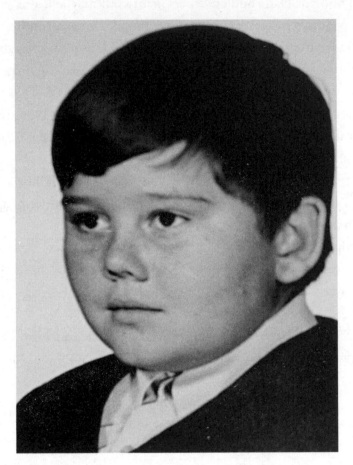

Young Louie

Tenth Child

Hey Mom,

It's me again, your tenth child, Louie, Louis Perry Anderson, as it states on my birth certificate, born March 24, 1953, at Ancker Hospital in St. Paul, Minnesota. Fatty Arbuckle's birthday. (I didn't know that then because I was just a baby.) You and Dad named me Louis after Dad, right? I mean, I'm not a Jr., because his and my middle names are different. But here's what I don't get: Why wait until the tenth kid and the fifth son before using Dad's name? Why not the firstborn male? Why eighteen years after you first became parents? I know my middle name is for your brother, Mom. You always talked so lovingly about Perry. Perry Prouty. I bet he got tortured over that name.

Here's the question people always ask me: What does it mean to be number ten of eleven? With nine older brothers and sisters and just one younger? Is there something particular about a family with eleven children? Some "eleven-ness"? Robert Kennedy Jr. is one of eleven children, so is Stephen Colbert, so is Mel Gibson. Do we all have something in common beyond just the number? I wonder if there's something similar between RFK Jr., Mel Gibson, Stephen Colbert, and me. I'm funny and Stephen Colbert is funny. Is Mel Gibson funny? Is RFK Jr.?

Do we tenth-borns have any special tendencies, the way firstborns might, or the baby of the family does, or the middle of three, or an only child? Does birth order matter that much? I have a book at home that's all about birth order, titled—what else?—*The Birth Order Book*, by Dr. Kevin Leman. The subtitle is *Why You Are the Way You Are*.

Is it that black-and-white? Does birth order determine everything? What number kid is it that never finishes reading books?

I always wondered if being your tenth, Mom, meant it was really hard for me to come across as special. You were forty-one years old when you had me. Like many moms back then, you got a week in the hospital, and having babies was your only real vacation. No wonder you had so many!

I'm glad I could give you that break—but it was the tenth such vacation. With nine children already, could number ten really seem special? I know when I see something over and over how it affects me. *Oh, another open mic comic. I've seen this before.* The tenth baby? Probably I was like that for you and Dad. Another mouth to feed, another round of diapers to change, another soft cherubic crying thing to hold and comfort, more money to earn and immediately spend. It must have been chaos at 1122 Hazelwood Street, the Roosevelt Projects on the East Side of St. Paul, Minnesota, before I showed up, and even more chaos afterward. So could I *really* have been special in some way? After all, not every comic is special. Brave, sure, and I have a lot of respect for what each comic is trying to do. But special? Most aren't. (Wait, is that me being judgmental? "I don't need to see that comic to know he's not special!")

Eventually, someone comes along who is special, like the first time I saw Jim Carrey. *Wow*, I remember thinking. *That's going to be a hard act to follow onstage.* At home I had nine acts to follow.

The only act that followed me was Tommy. I really wish I had asked you and Dad how it felt to bring home number ten.

When fans or interviewers ask, "What was it like growing up with ten brothers and sisters?" I never know how to answer it. By the time I arrived, the older ones were close to leaving the nest and very busy with their lives outside the home. There was the thing with Mary and, a decade after that, with Shanna, so not all of them were even there.

The middle kids helped take care of us younger ones, so to me and Tommy, the middle kids *were* the older kids. And the older kids were really adults.

What was it like growing up in a family that big? I had lots of examples of how to act, good and bad. We had only six chairs at the table, so we ate in shifts. There were two bathrooms, so we learned to control our bladders. The socks we wore were probably not ours.

Every family's circumstances are different. And I'm sure very big families are the same, in some ways. I wonder if Tolstoy is right, that happy families are happy in the same way but unhappy families are each unhappy in their own way. Oh, man, I would hate to try to figure that out. I know we had a lot of unhappiness. But were we unhappy in a unique way, or in a way very similar to other very big families? I ask too many damn questions. Anyway, Lisa probably said it best: "We made our own happiness but I don't think we were a happy family."

What were the reactions of Kent, Rhea, Mary, Roger, Jimmy, Shanna, Billy, Sheila, and Lisa to the ten-pound sack of potatoes carted into the Anderson Hacienda that March of '53? I'm going to make some calls, to three of my four remaining siblings, Mom, to get their impressions. (Not Tommy, since he wasn't born yet.

But I'll call him anyway, to say hi to my baby brother and tell him I love him.)

Four siblings. Yep, it's sad to say it. Jimmy, Shanna, Lisa, and Tommy. I have more to tell you about Kent, Rhea, Mary, Roger, Billy, and Sheila being gone, Mom, but later, not now. Just writing those words gets me emotional.

To be continued.

Love,

Louie

Premiere

Hey Mom,

I called Jimmy, your favorite child (admit it), and asked him what he thought of me when I came home from the hospital.

"I was excited but I don't know why," he said. Jimmy gets excited about everything. He always looks on the bright side. I don't know if he happens to be the best combination of you and Dad, or he arrived at just the right time, or it's birth order, or he was sunny-side up and I'm more of a hard-boiled egg. Anyway, that's Jimmy, pure and sweet, a sweetness he got from you, though he's also got a side of Dad's sour sauce.

Then I called Lisa but she didn't pick up.

Then I called Shanna, to see if she was even around when I was brought home from the hospital. Maybe she wasn't, maybe she was—that was years after you and Dad gave her away to be raised in a whole other state.

Shanna didn't pick up, so I left a message on her voice mail. Hey Mom, Shanna's living in your hometown of Mitchell, South Dakota. Home of the Corn Palace. Where you and Dad met. I think you know why she ended up back there.

Then Lisa called back. She said she remembers me coming home and she was super excited to see me, so excited that you let her hold me . . . and she dropped me on my head!

What?

Well, that explains everything, doesn't it, Mom? Dropped on the head. I didn't have a chance.

Being dropped on my head as a baby could explain my becoming a comedian. What's the right recipe for producing comedians—is it nice moms and mean dads? Mean moms and nice dads? Is that how you make the best comedians? I did a joke about the difference between moms and dads waking up their kids in the morning for school. Moms are usually so gentle and nice, even musical, sweetly letting you sink yourself because they seem content to say your name seven or eight hundred times. "Louie . . . oh, Lou-eee? . . . Louie, there's bacon and eggs, Louie . . . Louie, get up, everyone's waiting for you, Louie . . . I even have orange juice (remember, Mom, how we couldn't always afford orange juice?) . . . Louie, get up, please get up, Louie . . . LOOO-EE, I know you can hear me, Louie . . . Louie, sweetie? . . ."

Dads usually fire a warning shot or two. "Rise and shine!" "Hit the showers, then hit the road!" "Get up or your ass is grass!" "WAKE UP, DAMMIT!"

Seriously, Mom, I really do wish I knew what you and Dad thought of me when I entered this mad, mad, often really mean world.

Love,

Hardheaded Louie

Birthday Girl

Ora Zella

Mom

Hey Mom,

It's May 27, happy birthday! I won't say how old you'd be now because you never liked that. Who does, after thirty?

Sorry, Mom, actually I do need to share it. If I show these letters to anyone, they'll want to know. You were born in Mitchell, South

Dakota, 103 years ago, in 1912. I just looked up the *Argus-Leader*, the newspaper from nearby Sioux Falls, and that day it was in the mid-70s to low 80s. There were still front-page stories about the *Titanic*, which had sunk exactly six weeks earlier. William Howard Taft was president, our fattest, at 350 pounds.

You couldn't have been an easy birth because you were, like, a twelve-pound baby and your mom was such a tiny woman. That could explain the look on her face in those photographs. I wonder what your dad, Charlie, was doing when you were born. Was he at your mother's bedside, squeezing her hand, or at one of the gas stations he owned? What was he like? Like Roger? Like me? Like Dad, somehow? Maybe I'll call Aunt Shirley about the details. I never understood why we called her Aunt Shirley when she's a cousin. I should ask Aunt Shirley why we call her Aunt Shirley.

Who came up with your name, Ora Zella? That's a beauty, isn't it? It wasn't a very popular name—I looked it up. The top five girl names in 1912 were Mary, Helen, Dorothy, Margaret, and Ruth. There are lots of names in the Top 100 that year that you almost never hear anymore—Edna (#16), Bertha (#36), Fannie (#87), Velma (#88). But no Oras or Zellas among them. By the way, Mom, the top five girl names this year, 2015, are Sophia, Emma, Olivia, Ava, and Mia. Don't they sound like names from the past?

Did you know anyone with the name Ora? Did you like having an unusual name? What did they call you in school and at home?

I know Dad had a Scandinavian background—Swedish, Norwegian, English—and his childhood was so much more broken than yours. When his older sister Olga babysat while their parents were away, and then she threw a party, and that local Swedish gang showed up uninvited and killed someone, it was hard to blame the authorities for treating Dad's parents as unfit guardians, which led to the sad path his life took.

But do you think it would have been so, so different without that misfortune? I don't know. No one does.

You, on the other hand—you had a pretty good childhood! Your people go all the way back to the *Mayflower*. (How big was that boat, anyway?) You came from the Windsors, a prestigious name in British history. Do you know where your ancestors migrated to, and when? Did they hang out in Massachusetts for a while? Are you curious how they ended up in South Dakota?

I know you were born in Mitchell, S.D., in comfortable circumstances, to a mother and father you called "very loving parents." Your dad, Charles Prouty, owned filling stations, and you got to run the candy-and-cigarette stands. Al Capone once pulled into one of the stations, in a big, beautiful Packard, you told me, and gave the kid working the pump a twenty-dollar tip.

During the Depression, your dad extended credit to lots of customers but when the worst of it was over, many of them didn't pay him back. It broke his business, then his heart. I also heard, growing up, about how your dad got cheated out of some of his stations by a crooked lawyer.

So I'm confused, Mom. Did he die of a stroke—as I heard sometimes—or, as you often said, "a broken heart"? If it was a broken heart, was it from disappointment in his customers and the flaws of human nature, or because he got swindled? Or was the stroke the result of some other despair?

Even though he experienced disappointment in his financial and professional life, I wonder if it couldn't have been offset by the love he gave his wife and children, and that they gave him. Maybe Charles Prouty didn't see that as an equal trade.

I know you learned to drive a car at age thirteen and your dad got you a 1929 Buick, making you the only girl in town with her own car. How cool! Did that make you popular? Were you the most popular girl at school because you had your own car and your dad treated you like a queen? What's it like to be a popular teen? Good, I bet, really good. I wasn't the least popular kid in school but I wasn't the most popular, for sure, and I was usually picked last for teams, especially kickball. Gym was even less fun for me than it was for most kids. When you're a fat kid, you don't want to take your shirt off. Swimming, forget it.

But being the most popular, there's no way to go but down. Wherever we go in the world, there are very few Most Populars, and the rest of us have to share the crumbs left over from the baguette of life.

That makes my mouth water, Mom. Especially if there's a little dish of the butter of life.

So you were a girl in a small town, and Dad, my dad, was a trumpet player in a very successful band. His life was more dazzling but you had the car. And you thought he liked you. At least your car. Did you ever go with Dad to his gigs? He must have been great to listen to, and even to be around. Was he the only one you saw up on stage? When did the heavy drinking start? Did you see flashes of it and just tell yourself it was manageable? Was there *anything* he could have done right then, as you guys fell madly in love during the Depression, that would have made you walk away? You never gave up on him. Why is that? Was it love for him or just some Prouty sense of determination?

See, Mom: so many questions! Maybe too many. I'm so sorry now for those times I ever told you to shut up because you were going on and on, like on the thirteen-hour flight we took together to Europe.

Where do we get our strength from, Mom? From our parents? Or do we have it all along, inside us, and sometimes we just give others credit for it, even though they had little or nothing to do with it?

Boy, talk about people who need to shut up.

Love,

Louie

Dad, Mom, Uncle Perry under the tree, and a menagerie of Andersons

Training Day

Hey Mom,

On my flight today from Las Vegas to Los Angeles, they announced that they were training a pilot to become captain!

Who trains moms, Mom? Is it their mothers? How was your mom, Bertha, as a mom? Bertha Prouty—I don't even know her middle name. That's terrible. I should know more. Was she as loving as you? I doubt it. I met her. She lived with us a while. Why didn't I ask *her* everything?

Think of how much I lost by not asking all the questions I wanted. When do we lose that tendency? Because as kids we're constantly asking. *What is this for? Why? Mom, how did that baby get in your stomach? What color is water? Do ants poop? Do ants name their children? Why can't you toast salad? Where did grandpa go? Why do I sometimes get sad and start crying and don't know why? How? What? Why?* Kids know instinctively that asking questions helps them. They may not know consciously but they know that the answers will help them to understand the world and find their place in it and handle disappointment and money and success and the flu, and what to do with vegetable scraps and stale bread. Well, stale bread is easy. Just make stuffing with it or give it to your dad because he'll eat anything.

A question I wish I'd asked you, Mom: What the hell were you thinking marrying Dad?

Okay, I know. You got pregnant. Your parents weren't happy about it. You and Dad had to marry. That's what people did in the 1930s.

Still, if you said that was the reason you married Dad, I probably would have interrupted to say, "He was such a difficult man!"

No, that's not true. I would have said, "He was such a fricking difficult man!"

But was he as difficult back then?

I remember once asking you, "What did you see in him?"

"I loved his curls," you said. "He had beautiful curly hair."

I didn't comment on your answer then but I know what I would say now. "Oh, Mom, now I know where I get my shallowness!"

Sure, Dad was handsome. You were beautiful. Your father owned gas stations. You had a car. And Dad wanted a ride.

What I really should have asked you: "What the hell were you thinking having eleven children?"

People should ask their parents everything. But parents should also tell their kids everything. Would they even listen, though? Did I listen?

Ever-questioning,

Louie

A Dozen Questions Every Person Should Ask
Their Parent or Parents While They Still Can

1. Was your childhood a fairy tale, a drama, or a horror film?

2. What was your first thought when you two saw each other?

3. Why did you marry each other? Out of necessity? Were you lonesome?

4. What were you looking for in life? What did you feel you needed to do?

5. What did you already have, so you didn't need to look for it?

6. If you could live a do-over, what would it be? Would you change yourself or other things about your life?

7. What's the best thing you ever did besides have me?

8. If you could do three things to change the world, what would they be?

9. If you could have only one meal, would it be breakfast, lunch, or dinner?

10. What characters in movies were your mom and dad most like?

11. How did you know what I would like so much?

12. Tell me something you've never told anyone.

Silent Dancing

Hey Mom,

We did this thing that's pretty cool, I think. Remember "silent dance" parties, where everyone on the dance floor wears headphones and listens to the same music and dances to it, but there's no music outside? Wait, no, actually you wouldn't—that's not even my generation! I don't know whose generation it is, the one after mine, or the current one. Anyway, silent dance parties. (I can hear Dad raising his voice: "What the hell will they think of next—silent screaming?") So that idea gave me this one: What if we transmitted the audio of one of my Vegas stand-up shows, live, to the local VA hospital, and all the injured and recovering vets who want can listen to it on headphones, and there would be laughter throughout the building? I sure hope there would be laughter.

They did it, Mom! We did it! At the Las Vegas VA hospital. I wish I could have heard it and seen it myself but I was onstage performing live what they were listening to. Hey Mom: If you tell a joke and no one's listening, does that mean it isn't funny?

I'll get a chance to meet some of the vets next week, when I go to the hospital for a "meet and greet."

We need to do more of that. I want to get other entertainers to join. Why don't we all make a better effort to treat our veterans like we do our loved ones?

On second thought, given some families, that wouldn't be such a great idea.

Love,

Proud son of a war veteran, Louie

You and Me

Hey Mom,

Remember when we would venture out early Saturday morning to Flying Cloud Airport, just you and me, for the flea market? Most times it was a quiet ride there, with our packed boxes in the back of the big Buick. Sometimes it was a pleasant mother-son conversation. Once, we fantasized that a rich antiques dealer from California was going to stop by our booth of pottery, glassware, and jewelry, surveying the "treasures" (your word; "junk," Dad's word), and then, with a sudden magical sweep of his arm, the dealer would say, "I'll take it all!" Then he'd unsnap his fancy alligator wallet and open it up to reveal a thick wad of hundreds, to your amazement and my teenage giggles.

"Wouldn't that be a nice break, Louie?" you said.

And we really could have used one, especially after the previous night, like so many others, we'd had with the maniac.

The real flea market experience was never like that, of course. Not only did we not make a killing, we never made *any* money. You priced everything too high because you had no real intention of selling. "Oh, that's not supposed to be out there! That's not for sale. I'm keeping that!" Instead, while I unfolded our table and unpacked our boxes, you walked around the market, buying things. Everybody there knew you, everybody liked you. You'd come back ten minutes later with one or two or four items. "Look at this cruet, Louie. It's an oil and vinegar cruet. It has a couple chips in it, but for two dollars, how could I go wrong?" I was still unpacking and we were already in the hole. And that's not even including the gas it took to get down there.

We always returned home with more than what we came with.

I realized much later it was not about selling, it was about us spending time together.

Unsaid no more,

Louie

Daily Prayer

Hey Mom,

I wasn't doing this back when you were around but these days I start my day by praising God and praying for everybody I know. I ask for forgiveness for all those I've hurt. I want to be bighearted. Mom, I learned this from you. You were always bighearted toward Dad despite all the things he did to you. You still forgave him, still loved him. Was that a defect in you or grace from God? Anyway, I try to start my day outside myself, so I don't go crazy. I should honor something other than myself first. I find it's helpful. Sometimes I'll do my prayers before getting out of bed, sometimes I'll make my bed first and then do my prayers. I'll say what I have to say out loud. Then I get ready for the day, the kind of place I need to be. If I know I'll be running in circles most of the day, it's good to prepare for that. Then again, it's never good to run in circles because you always end up right where you are. You should run in a direction that brings you in touch with a new way of life, a new world, new people. So many people today run in circles, Mom, more than they used to, it seems. I don't want to be like that. Maybe I'll start running in ovals.

I don't know if it's right to pray for things like professional success. Maybe it's the opposite of honoring something besides yourself. But now and then, I confess, I have prayed for work that is really, truly fulfilling, not just for my benefit but so that people have a chance to see what I'm really capable of. I'm not just this comic doing fat jokes. In my life right now I think I finally have a deep understanding of humanity and my soul. You're the genesis of that, Mom. And if you're the genesis, Dad's the Deuteronomy. I don't know what that means, Mom, but you gotta admit, Deuteronomy's a funny word.

So I do my daily prayers, then make some coffee and eat my food. Food doesn't become the most important thing to me. I try to make it more ritual than reward.

Trying to run in a straight line,

Louie

The Hair Twirlers

Hey Mom,

Were you a hair twirler?

Remember when Billy twirled his hair? I thought it was a weird habit but lots of people do it and here's my theory: hair twirling isn't just a physical tic but a mechanism to cope with stress or the other upsetting thoughts in our noggins. It's what you do when you can't tell the world what you're thinking. *I'm so fricking crazy, nobody knows it but me, I wish I could get them to lower the lights in this room, I wish the phone would ring, I'm crazy . . .*

Billy always twirled his hair. God, I miss him. He was a lovely human being.

I had hair twirlers sitting in front of me on each of my last two flights. The woman in front of me on my flight to Omaha (on my way to perform at the Great American Comedy Festival in Norfolk, Nebraska, childhood home of Johnny Carson)—she was twirl and untwirl, twirl and untwirl, twirl, untwirl. *I wish I could get this flight to be over already* is my guess. Maybe she was thinking something else.

Doesn't everyone know a hair twirler? If they don't, they should find one.

The hair twirlers on my flights made it through okay. Thank God they had hair. What about hair twirlers who happen to be bald? Do they twirl their children's hair?

I wish Billy knew things could be okay. But he was afraid. He was paranoid. Who was trying to get him?

Was Billy always a little different? No one knew it when they first met him. He was so good-looking, like one of the Kennedys, and people talked to him for a little while and probably went, *Okay*, but then Billy would say something, like, *Hey, those people over there are taking pictures of us*, and the person he was talking to would say, *But they don't even have a camera*, and Billy would say, *Their glasses are cameras*. Or he'd say, *What are you looking at?* And they were looking at nothing, certainly not at him. He loved adventure, and hunted for gold and diamonds. Then again, he could get upset over something, storm out, and not return for a couple years.

But if Billy were alive today, in this day and age, he'd probably be one of those people to invent the next big thing. He was a dreamer and a schemer. He gave me some of my best ideas. He wanted me to come out with Louie's Extra Sugar Louie Gooey Candies. "Be sure to say *extra* sugar," he said. "It's the extra that makes it."

He was so right. William David Anderson. My brother Billy. Hair twirler extraordinaire.

Was I ever a twirler? I remember when I got really worried, I would take out a deck of playing cards and turn them over one by one, and if I got more aces and face cards than number cards I felt better about things. How crazy is that, Mom? A queen, a jack—my day is going to be just fine!

I don't do cards anymore. Today, I try to deal with my anxiety and insecurity by taking a deep breath and saying a prayer and knowing that I'm strong enough and brave enough to handle anything that comes my way.

Mom, you used to rub your right hand up and down your

left arm, probably to comfort yourself or to find something, your way of saying to yourself, *Everything is going to be all right.* When Dad would have one of his episodes, I remember you going to the kitchen sink, turning on the faucet, and washing your hands. Or sometimes you'd straighten and smooth the doilies on the sofa over and over again, even when they were already as straight and smooth as could be.

You know what, Mom? You were pretty much a hair twirler, too.

Love,

Louie

Finding Ora

Hey Mom!

We just started filming the first season of *Baskets*, and already it might be the most creative adventure of my life. Christine Baskets is pretty important to the show and if this thing takes off, or at least holds on, I can honestly say that it's not just me you're keeping in a job, it's other people in their jobs, too. Nice trick considering you passed away a quarter-century ago.

Okay, I can see where that might sound big-headed. There are quite a few creative geniuses I'm working with who have a huge impact on what happens with our show.

So, how I got the job:

I've been in Vegas for about eleven years now. I'm not sure if it's eleven. I'm terrible with dates. In fact, I often forget the birthdays and birth years of some of my sisters and brothers. Maybe it's forgivable when you have ten to remember. I'm digressing again, Mom. Anyway, I moved there ten or eleven years ago and got a job at the Excalibur Hotel and Casino, in the old Catch a Rising Star room. For the next half a decade, I did five to six nights a week there, then moved for three years to the Palace Station (playing at the—what else?—"Louie Anderson Theater"), then headed downtown to the Plaza Hotel and Casino, where I'd been for about a year when I was heading to work one day and my cell phone rang. (Yes, Mom, people now carry their phones with them. More on that later.) It was my agent calling. He said that Louis C.K. needed my number.

A couple minutes later, he called.

"Hey, Louie," said Louie.

"Hey, Louie," I said.

"I'm with Zach Galifianakis," he said. "We're doing a new show and we'd like you to play a part."

In less time than it takes to say "Yes!" I said, "Yesssss!"

I didn't need to know what the part was or the show. Zach Galifianakis is a great comic actor and an excellent serious actor, too, a creative genius. Mom, he looks like Billy with a beard. And Louis C.K.'s TV show had won a couple Emmy Awards and been nominated for many more.

Then Louis told me, "We want you to play Zach's mom."

Immediately I said, "Yesssss!"

Zach said that when he was considering who he wanted to play the mother of his characters—he plays identical twins—the one thing he knew was that the mom made a nasal, Midwestern sound sort of like "Aaaaaaaah . . ."

Which made Louis C.K. say, "You mean, like Louie Anderson?"

"Yeah, like Louie Anderson," said Zach.

Remember, Mom, how I said I sometimes prayed for a job like this? Those prayers were answered.

As soon as the call was over, I looked up and said, "Hey Mom, what do you think? You're finally going to be in show business. I hope I do you justice." I was surprisingly calm about this call that might change my life, and the challenge of the role. But I was Mr. Cool because, hey, in my act I'd been doing your voice and facial expressions forever, Mom.

The idea of playing a woman didn't faze me at all. I grew up with five sisters. Once, I played a maid in a scene with Dom Irrera, for his comedy special, the only time I could remember playing in drag. But from what they had told me about *Baskets*, I didn't look at this as drag. The character would just be real.

It was months before I got a call about shooting the pilot. I was given an address in Sylmar. That's California, Mom, in the Valley. Anyway, I got there and in a gigantic trailer, I put on the clothes they had for me. I don't know if it was a skirt or slacks. It was still dark when I arrived and I wasn't quite awake. TV and movie shoot hours are very different from live comedy show hours. After I got dressed I went to another trailer, where they put makeup on me, then I moved over to the hair person, who put a wig on me, then back to the makeup person, who put lipstick on me. There's something about putting lipstick on when you're facing the mirror, even if someone else applies it for you. You can't not purse your lips, kind of pucker them, and say to yourself, maybe even out loud, "Hey, I look pretty good!"

To be honest, Mom, I was nervous as we took a shuttle van up to the set, which was kind of a cute, ticky-tacky row house. I had already met the cast, the director, the writers—Zach, who's an exceptionally nice guy; Martha Kelly, a very talented stand-up who's one of the main characters; Jonathan Krisel, one of the show's co-creators and lone director. I loved the script and I'd been thinking a lot about how I was going to play Christine. Now, to Jonathan, who also seemed very sweet, I said, "Hey, I'm not gonna change my voice for this character."

My voice can get up there but, honestly, it's pretty deep.

He thought about it for a moment. "Okay," he said.

I was going to play this woman in my own voice. Because I wanted to do as little "make-believe" as possible.

Throughout the filming of the pilot, Jonathan's direction was always smart and sensitive and minimal. I could tell he had very specific things in mind but he wouldn't ever push you to do it his way. He would never say a take wasn't good. He would say, "Why don't we try it . . . ?" and then give a word or two that nudged it in a different direction. Sometimes I would say to him, "Can I just say it how my mom would?"

He always said yes. And it always worked best that way, for everybody. I had so much fun playing this lovely mother.

Christine Baskets actually has two sets of twins, the pair Zach plays—Chip and Dale—and an adopted pair, Cody and Logan. Not quite eleven children but still a handful, even though they are supposedly grown-ups. Mom, you were pregnant with twins, twice, but miscarried both times. That must have been so sad for you. I love you, Mom. I'm so sorry.

(Wow. That could have been fifteen kids. Makes eleven look like child's play.)

Hey Mom, remember the Wonder Bread store where we used to buy day-old bread, ten loaves for a dollar? God, how crazy was that? Those cinnamon buns. I always wanted the cinnamon buns, and cookies by the bin for a dollar. I loved that. That was a real high for me. I can still smell those rolls and those cookies, hold on, I gotta lie down for a minute. I'm kidding. Anyway, I bring it up because Costco (Mom, were they around and popular before you died in 1990? I'm not sure. I'll check. But they're a big big-box store chain. Did we use the phrase "big-box store" when you were around? I don't know, I'll check), anyway Costco, which is like our Gem Store, the everything store especially for veterans, anyway Costco (can I go even thirty seconds without breaking off for a tangent? Can I be serious for thirty seconds? What fun is that?), ANYWAY COSTCO let us, the *Baskets* show, use their Kirkland brand products in the kitchen. So the kitchen on set was overflowing with cinnamon rolls, bread, just about every delicious fattening food you could think of. And as soon as I walked into that kitchen, I thought of the day-old store. Was it a Wonder Bread store or a Gold Medal Flour store? I entertained the cast and crew with ways you might describe all that bread and those muffins and stuff courtesy of Kirkland and Costco. Remember how you used adjectives for food that are usually applied to works in a museum? "Did you ever see a more beautiful muffin? . . . How about those donut holes? Jeez, they're like pieces of art. . . . Look at the swirl on this cinnamon toast—if it isn't a Picasso, I don't know what is."

Then we filmed a whole scene about a Costco product, a scene that called for me to drink a whole can of Kirkland brand sports drink. I got about halfway through and knew I wasn't going to make it, so I spit some out and tried to save the scene. I ad-libbed, "Oh, that was refreshing" or "Oh, that hit the spot," something understated, and wouldn't you know? We used the whole take in the episode! I guess that's what they *really* mean in show business by "the spit take."

Sometimes mistakes make for the best scenes.

After we shot the pilot, I heard nothing for a long time. I was really hoping to play the part again but I didn't know if the show would get the green light. (That's a Hollywood expression, Mom. It's also a traffic expression.) Yes, our show had known comedy names "attached" to it, which really helps, but you never know with Hollywood. You don't.

Then one beautiful day I got the call that the FX network had committed to a ten-episode season of *Baskets*. (Thank you, FX!) It's a bittersweet comedy. Jonathan calls it a "slapstick drama." He's a genius, I think, really special. I learned about complimenting people from you, Mother, you're the master at it (that's not to say I'm being insincere in what I just said about Jonathan). You made people feel better all the time. I keep that tradition going for you. I try to make people feel good. I ask the crew and other cast members real questions about themselves and their families and their partners and their career hopes and dreams, and I don't shy away from discussing hardships and disappointments. I would call you a "super-communicator," Mom. You really knew how to connect with people. And you passed it on to me—though I'm a big ham on top of it. You were funny, too, Mom, very funny, actually.

At the beginning of the first season, Jonathan said something smart: Don't think of this as ten episodes but as a three-and-a-half-hour movie, the whole season. That gives it a sense of an arc, like it's moving toward something clear, not just going on and on, driven by ratings and how many seasons we get renewed.

I wonder how many people look at their own lives as having an arc, and live their lives accordingly, given the built-in certainty of cancellation. We're all going to get canceled someday. We just don't know how many seasons we'll be around for.

Baskets is scheduled to premiere early next year but I'm not thinking yet about the reaction. I'm having too much fun.

I love playing you, Mom. It feels so natural. Maybe it will help me understand you even more. What you had to put up with.

Love,

Louie

One Thing I Really Miss

Hey Mom,

Being in the kitchen with you when you were making something delicious—how great was that?

Dad wasn't home from work yet. No one else was there—well, maybe Lisa, she was always helpful, but often it was just you and me. You'd begin the ritual of taking all the vegetables out and cleaning them. "I hate dirty celery," you'd say. "Celery should be clean and crisp." You'd cut them precisely, each piece the size of knuckles, then wash the radishes, then cut them in half. You loved radishes. You loved a good cucumber. "Peel a cuke for me, Louie." You'd put them in vinegar and cut up onions and let them marinate. As delicious as they were then, when I think about them now they seem even more so, because the older we get, the more we like things pickled. Dad was always pickled, wasn't he, Mom?

"That was a good one, Louie!"

What a good laugh you had! You'd keep cutting vegetables and you'd purse your lips and your eyes would go up, the same expression Christine uses. It comes close to looking like exasperation but it's not. It's satisfaction. It's approval.

"That was a good one, Louie."

Then you'd say, "Louie, grab that roast—isn't that a gorgeous roast?" I never thought a word like "gorgeous" applied to something like a roast but you did, maybe because you knew how to make anything beautiful and valuable, the way you made us feel safe no matter how much danger we were living in.

The way you set the table, you'd think the President was coming over. Little salt dips for the radishes, oil and vinegar cruets, cloth napkins. If for no one else, Mom, at least it was for you. You found a way to live richly in poor conditions. High-class all the way.

I miss those little things—but now I don't really have to miss them because I reenact them on TV.

Love,

Louie

Each Parent Got a Book

Hey Mom,

We have a break in filming *Baskets*, so I'm doing a few dates in the Midwest—Traverse City, Michigan, and Worthington, Minnesota. At my last couple of shows, several people came up to me to talk about my book about Dad. It's been almost thirty years since it was published but it really strikes a nerve with some people.

When *Dear Dad* came out I received more than ten thousand letters, letters that were really emotional, sometimes heartbreaking, from readers who felt as if they were reading their own story in my struggle to understand a difficult, frequently cruel alcoholic parent. One letter writer actually visited Dad's gravesite, at Fort Snelling National Cemetery, just like I did at the end of the book. "I hope you don't mind," the person wrote. "I felt very close to you and your family after reading your book."

Mind? How could I mind? It was a beautiful sentiment. It's comforting to find others like me. Alcoholism is a silent assassin that keeps attacking long after the attacker is dead and gone. We keep feeling it. Forever. Trauma is trauma, Momma, and I thank you for standing in front of the blast, time and again.

Another letter writer wrote that, in the same way Dad was with us, his father "never told me anything at all about his childhood, and I thought that odd. People from that generation were different. Their lives were different. The world also was different."

That's true. Dad's unwillingness to share moments from his terrible childhood and from the war—a lot of that could have as much to do with generational style as with who he was or what he suffered. Or maybe it comes down to a really simple idea: Who wants to revisit the scene of a crime? Who wants to revisit what they felt they had laid to rest? But you know, Mom, it's always right there, the source of the pain. It's right there, within reach. You have to stare it down, back it into a corner, say, *You have no power over me*, until the monster is no longer a monster, it's just a little pea in a pod and that little pea can't affect you anymore. Only fear and anxiety allow the pea to grow into a boulder.

Another letter writer, David, a self-described "fat ACOA," wrote that "Your life and mine have taken different paths, but the feelings you describe are the same as mine. I am tempted to send the book to my father. Maybe I will." I hope he did. On the other hand, a letter writer from Massachusetts wrote, "You're looking for answers, Louie, but there might not be any." If she's right, that will be very frustrating. But she's probably right. Right?

Am I supposed to stop asking questions?

One letter writer asked a question about his recently deceased alcoholic father that I never asked of Dad, but now I'm obsessed with it: "I could not help wondering, *What was it like at the moment of that last heartbeat? What was his very last thought?*"

Me too. Was Dad's last thought, *Hey, I'd love to have one more drink*?

Was it, *I'm sorry*?

Was it, *Ah, shit . . . that's* IT?

Maybe the last thought was relief from a lifelong fight with his own demons and dragons. His boulder. His mother and father. His father's father. Maybe it was memories of a childhood whose chance for more happiness ended so abruptly.

One twenty-one-year-old woman, with a double whammy—*both* parents were alcoholic—wrote to me, "The big thing that I am not getting over is the guilt and self-esteem thing. I can't think of myself as worthwhile although I'm ready to. I have had enough of this life."

This woman has a baby son. She sells shoes at Sears, in a mall. She has struggled with food and weight issues, too, bulimic for years. Her husband is a recovering alcoholic. Her father is in denial about his alcoholism.

Yet she writes to me things like, "I really want to tell you about [my husband's] relapse. It's the kind of morbid-funny humor you might like." And "I've been in treatment and everything—it's all really laughable!"

Isn't that remarkable, Mom? How can people still do that, after so much pain?

I think part of us becomes addicted to the dread, the drama, the disrespect. We crave it, we need it, we search for it in others and in ourselves. But there's a switch you have to learn how to turn off, a "discomfort switch"—*At least I know I'm no good. At least I know they hate me. At least things are not going to work out.* That switch has to be turned off. Sometimes we need to just find an actual switch in the house and turn it off. Any switch. Just find one. Turn it off and say, *I'm worth it I'm worth it I'm worth it I'm worth it worth it worth it.* We may have to say it a few thousand times before we start to believe it.

I'm worth it, Mom, and so were you.

Love,

Louie

Life Sucks Without Bread

Hey Mom,

Did you know that Minnesota has the world's largest candy store?

I thought I might get a chance to go there on this trip home but it doesn't look like it. I've never been there but I'm proud that Minnesota's Largest Candy Store, in Jordan, just south of Chaska, is also supposedly the *world's* largest candy store. (Mom, we also have the largest shopping mall in the country, the Mall of America. It opened in Bloomington two years after you died. It gets about the same number of visitors every year as Disneyland, Disney World, Yellowstone, and Yosemite combined. You would have been a regular.)

I remember buying candy as a kid. I got money from you or Dad and went to the corner store by school and bought "silver dollars," two for a penny—red licorice in the shape of a half-dollar piece, hard and delicious. I'd cram them into my mouth, systematically feed them in as if my mouth were a vending machine. And even when it got full, I'd keep at it and usually jam the slot. And I would just keep chewing and chewing and slowly chewing. I remember my jaw would be so sore because I had to finish the candy before I got home or to school. Maybe I even drooled some, in my lust to eat and finish. I've forgotten lots of things from my childhood but I remember that exact feeling.

Is that food addiction? Probably. After all, I'm a food addict.

You know what's amazing? Even as I write this, I really can feel it in my jaw. The insatiable need for that candy, or really any food, that feeling that I *shouldn't* have. That feeling, oh my God I have to have this I will even steal money out of my dad's pants dig for pennies so I can get that candy. That was my first drug of choice, candy. There was a secret involved. There was shame involved. I was trying to hide it from others. What was going on with me, Mom? What exactly happened to me? Why was I somehow able to take that terrible drawback and cultivate it into a successful career as a comedian?

Because that's what I did: I turned it all around. I turned it on its head. I used it against myself so that people couldn't use it against me. I took charge of it. Of the knowledge. *I* could dole out however much I wanted. I was the controller over myself.

Wow, that's a little heartbreaking.

At meals I had to be careful about how much food I put on my plate because Dad was watching and he might yell at me for how much I took. "Lard ass" was the go-to insult.

But you gotta have enough mashed potatoes so you can make an indentation deep enough for the gravy to pool.

And you need the corn.

And the pot roast, Mom, which you had been cooking for three or four hundred hours—wouldn't it be rude not to have seconds? When there are people in Africa and China way poorer than even us who could never afford such a meal? Oh, and you have to take some more of that incredibly delicious gravy, which is meant for the pot roast anyway, so it wouldn't be right to have pot roast *without* gravy. (At Thanksgiving, you would make seven thousand pounds of sweet potatoes, then you would ask periodically, "Did you have some sweet potatoes?" Of course I had but whenever you asked that, how could I not take another helping? Especially when you said, "They're hot. There's more in the oven. There's some in the garage." That last part I made up.)

And the hot buns.

And the iceberg lettuce, which doubled as a healthy Anderson salad.

And there was always dessert.

And we had our own deep fryer.

When we first got the deep fryer, I remember that we cut up every potato we could find to make french fries. You have to. Then we got more sophisticated and made potato chips, all by hand— we didn't have any kind of slicer. We were the slicers and dicers. Then we took chicken to fry up but we never really knew what we were doing with chicken. At least I didn't. We wanted to fry up anything—onion rings, of course, and a whole can of that white lard you used so often, Mom. I thought about throwing a potholder into the fryer to see if it would crisp.

We all have our own drug. Mine is food. It was for you, too, Mom, though maybe not quite as much. The few photographs I've seen of you as a child show a plump little girl. And only two of the eleven Anderson kids are, or were, what you could actually call thin. The other nine are, or were, anywhere from slightly over-weight to obese to morbidly obese, like Mary and me. Tommy gets up there, too, though he was fat in a different way, "big boned," a bigger skeleton than mine, built more like Dad. I'm built more like you, Mom, with a smaller skeleton. My fat all pools in the gut and the thighs.

In one way, food is a tougher drug to deal with than actual drugs. In some ways. Not in other ways. For a lot of people it's still hard to believe that food is a drug. But just like other drugs, it affects us emotionally *and* physiologically. When I bite into a Carl's Jr. six-dollar burger, I have a physiological reaction to it, which then alters me emotionally. Maybe the high isn't as big as the high from cocaine, say, but it certainly changes how I feel. *I'm okay now, I'm okay now, I'm okay now.*

The other night I had some bread. Now, Mom, I'm trying to not eat bread these days, so that's got to be something of a surprise to you. But the restaurant had gluten-free bread and I knew I could have that. Gluten-free bread has no wheat and it's the wheat that really affects me. So I took some lean turkey, put it on the gluten-free bread, bit into it and I was like, *Oh, I get it—It's not just gluten-free but taste-free, too!* So disappointing. The only way to eat gluten-free bread is to toast it, butter it real good, then put jam on it, until you've eliminated the whole point of the gluten-freedom.

And here's why in some ways food's the hardest addiction: food addicts can't ever completely avoid their weakness. We need food to live. Yes, I should eat healthy, organic, fresh, non-processed food . . . but I'm still always skirting disaster. You don't tell a crackhead they can still go to the crack den, just don't have any crack. When I drive past a McDonald's, am I supposed to pretend I don't see the golden arches? Pretend it's just a yellow statue of butt cheeks and move on?

AND HOW MUCH STEAMED BROCCOLI CAN ONE MAN EAT??!

Sometimes it feels as if the only thing I'm allowed to eat is steam. Eventually I would like some cheddar cheese in my steam.

I try to eat healthier, Mom, but I came from an unhealthy family. And I still feel as if healthy food has a ways to go.

"How much are the organic bananas?"

"Two ninety-nine a pound."

"And the non-organic bananas?"

"They're free."

"Give me the free bananas and some organic stickers."

I have trouble with some of the other labeling, too, like "free-range." What does that mean? It means that instead of being cooped up before we kill them, the chickens get to run free before we kill them. But you know the cooped-up chickens are trying to warn the free-range chickens, sticking their heads up against the wire windows, calling out, "You're living a lie, Betty!"

Actually, it's not food that's my drug. It's bread. Life really sucks without bread. It does. Growing up Anderson, it felt like, if there's no bread, there's no meal. Here, today, I was having a great day, Mom, I took care of myself, I exercised, I ate healthy, then I went to meet some friends at a restaurant and they brought us a loaf of really, really good Italian bread with an incredible crust . . . If I were put on a desert island, I would just want a giant baguette and a keg of butter. That sounds so great, actually. I bet you think so, too, Mom. Remember I used to joke about how "my mom ate every piece of butter in the Midwest"?

I had a dream the other night that I had died. I was taken to the funeral home and they embalmed me with butter. When they went to place me in the casket, it was a giant baguette. They slid me in, cut a hole in the top, and a breadstick was holding the top of the casket open. People were walking by me, paying their respects and saying, "God, he smells good." One person even grabbed a hunk of the baguette casket as they walked by. The only problem is, they left my shoes on. If you're going to slide me into a baguette casket, remove my shoes.

Life sucks without bread.

Warmly, with butter,

Louie

Louie Anderson Is Dead

Hey Mom,

When we finish filming Season 1 of *Baskets*, I'm sure I'll feel a little let down. Hopefully we'll get renewed for a second season, but either way, I'm grateful for the experience. I try to appreciate every moment. You never know when you won't be able to anymore.

I was dead, once, for a few hours.

About six years ago, some jokers decided to pull a hoax that I had died. Not just me but Britney Spears, Jeff Goldblum, Harrison Ford, George Clooney, Miley Cyrus, Natalie Portman, and Ellen DeGeneres, too. We had all died. The idea was to spread the news on the Internet. (What's the Internet, Mom? Okay, it's basically the world now, the "place" where we spend most of our waking hours, even though it's not really real, or it *is* real but most of us don't know where it is. It's a place where you can do lots of things, including things you didn't even particularly want to do, and learn odd things, like that you're dead when you're not. It's just like the actual world, Mom—hard to explain.) I can't remember the cause of my death but Jeff allegedly fell from a sixty-foot cliff while filming a movie in New Zealand; Harrison allegedly drowned in a capsized yacht in the Riviera; and George allegedly died in a private-plane crash in Colorado. So I was dead, we were dead, to at least a bunch of strangers, until we started piping up that we weren't. I don't know how many people have to believe a hoax for it to be considered a success, but for a while, if you googled "Louie Anderson," maybe the fourth entry that came up was "Louie Anderson is dead." (What's Google, Mom? You know when you couldn't remember some actor's name or the name of the shopping center with the Red Owl grocery, and you'd call your friend Monny because she always knew all that stuff, or you could remember only the names of two of the ships that Columbus sailed, the *Niña* and the *Pinta*, but not the third? Well, imagine there's a place you can type in your questions, and you don't even have to type them in question form, just use a few key words, and suddenly, before you can even get your eyeglasses on, it's telling you that it was Robert Mitchum, Phalen Shopping Center, or the *Santa Maria*. That's what Google is—a thousand Monnys out there and more, millions of them. Google is the person in the neighborhood with all that information, like Monny, but also the nosiest person, kind of like Darlene. You remember Darlene, Mom? Three doors down, always had her nose out the window? Because not only is Google answering your questions but then it's getting inside your head to figure out what you might think of next before you think of it. Were you asking about sparkly shoes? The next time you go on your computer, you'll see an ad to buy sparkly shoes. So it's sort of like Monny times a million plus Darlene, if Darlene were Big Brother.)

Anyway, when the hoax about my death turned out to be just a hoax, lots of people on Twitter tweeted me, *Louie, I thought you were dead*, and I would reply, *Hold on, let me check*. I guess I can't be that mad at the hoaxers because I got a rare gift: the chance to experience what it's like to have people think you're dead, then they realize no, you're not, then you enjoy this outpouring of genuine feeling and relief, with them calling or writing to say, "Oh, Louie,

I'm so happy you're still alive!" Me too! I liked being dead for a little while. Kind of like Tom and Huck standing at the back of the church listening to their own eulogies and the whole town weeping for them.

(This is Twitter, Mom: Imagine you're in class and you write a note that says "I like your new shoes," and pass it to your friend Ruthie, and Ruthie writes something on the note but instead of passing it back to you she passes it to someone else, and it goes around the room, and when it finally gets back to you, your note not only says "Thank you" from Ruthie but it also has a lot of comments from classmates saying that they love her shoes, some that say they hate her shoes, and also some mean comments about you, from classmates who don't really know you that well. And while the comments are all signed, some of them have names that are clearly made up, like ImAnIdiot or RobinsonCrusoe3rd or SoHungry. Mom, here's the thing about the Internet, Google, Twitter, and a lot of other inventions that weren't around when you were: they're all versions of things that existed only we've added electricity to them, which in some ways made them better and in other ways ruined them.)

One nice thing about coming back to life is lots of people got back in touch with me.

Louie Anderson is not dead.

I want to be with you, Mom, I really do.

Just not yet.

Still kicking,

Louie

P.S. I'll write to you about the day you died, for real. Just not yet.

No Family Feud

Hey Mom,

   If I didn't have you as a model, I wouldn't have had success playing the matriarch of a dysfunctional but ultimately loving TV family. I've been thinking about that, and about how art imitates life. And how my real family has influenced not only who I am but my professional success, too. I mean, I do lots of material about the family. My TV cartoon, *Life with Louie*, was our life, barely disguised. I worked on another TV show, a sitcom, *The Johnsons Are Home*, also based on our family. Then there's *Family Feud*, the incredibly popular game show that has "family" in the very title and turned out to be this weird, joyous thread throughout my life.

   Do you remember our watching *Family Feud* when I was still living at home, with you and Dad, Tommy was still there, too, and Tommy and I sat on the couch, or I sat on the arm of the couch, and maybe Tommy wasn't there but upstairs in the bedroom, looking through my record albums? Anyway, Dad was in his chair, and you were in the kitchen, and like every American family we tried to guess the number one answer, and you would come out of the kitchen occasionally and throw your two cents in. Dad would complain about Richard Dawson slobbering over the women when he kissed them. I think Dad might have been jealous.

   About twenty-five years later, the producers of *Family Feud* were looking for a new host and they wanted me to do a pilot, but I wouldn't. I knew that if you shoot a pilot, afterward they can easily say, Uh . . . no, and if they *really* want you, they'll put up the money to attract you. Hire you for the job or not.

So we didn't shoot a pilot. (I'm not a terrorist, Mom.) But the producers asked if I would go to London to host some episodes of *Family Fortunes*, the British version of *Family Feud*, and I went, and the contestants were American servicemen and servicewomen stationed over there, and the producers thought I was terrible. I probably was.

Oh, well.

But when I was back doing shows in Vegas, the producers asked if I would host an episode, taping it with audience members onstage, as a sales tool to show to station managers across the country. It so happened that we were having an Anderson family reunion in Vegas right around that time, and we could be the guests, on both sides! So we did. I played host with both sides of the family—brothers and sisters, nieces and nephews—and it was so much fun. And because I was so relaxed—*my* family! battling it out on *Family Feud*!—the tape of that episode landed me the job as the new host, though that wasn't even the point!

Some people who care about me wondered why I would take the job. They said it would hurt my career. I said, "Well, let's see, my comedy is all about my family, I did a cartoon about my family, why *wouldn't* I do *Family Feud*?" I'm glad I listened to myself. I wasn't afraid that I couldn't do this or that. I don't think it hurt my career. I think it helped it. I learned a great deal doing it. And those were three of the most fun years of my life, from 1999 through 2001. I wish you could have seen it, Mom. You would have been calling answers out at the TV, with your second-youngest child on just the other side of the screen to tell you and everyone else what the survey said. I love game shows. They're part of America. I like to think we invented them but I have no idea if we did.

We shot five shows a day, and filmed on thirty-six days, so in a little more than a month's worth of shooting we completed 180 shows, a year's worth (each show runs twice). First we did it at CBS, in the same studio where they filmed *The Price Is Right*, then moved to NBC, where they filmed *The Tonight Show*. How great is that? The ratings for the show reversed their downward trend. They doubled, in fact.

Then, somewhere along the way, I got really full of myself.

I wish I would have worked harder at that point in my career, and been nicer. The show's success made me think it would just go and go and go. But that's not how life happens, I learned. I acted like a big shot. People kept telling me how great I was, and guess what? I believed them! I sometimes acted rude and mean, like a prima donna. I could be difficult. I hurt people and I regret that. I hurt myself, too. I tripped on myself, Mom. I didn't even see it. And so life and success didn't just go and go and go. It was go and go and . . . gone. After the third season, they replaced me. I was devastated. I didn't know what to do. Because I wasn't good with my money, I had to relocate from L.A. to Las Vegas. Eventually I landed a great gig there with Spy Entertainment, at the Excalibur, and Las Vegas saved me. I worked a regular show in Vegas for more than a decade.

I learned a lot from that painful period in my life. Do we learn much from the painless periods?

Wondering,

Louie

That's Somebody's Baby

Hey Mom,

This past Thursday night I was coming out of a charity event in Hollywood. As I reached the corner where a car was waiting for me, I noticed a big plastic cup perched in front of a yellow blanket, the kind of blanket we grew up with, fuzzy with silk trim, the type we had on our beds and built forts with and spread out on lawns on the night of July Fourth to watch fireworks. Anyway, it took me a moment to realize what I was looking at. At first it was just a blanket on the sidewalk. But wait, no, it was twisted in such a way that it looked almost like a partial chalk outline of a murder scene, with a pair of footed white tube socks peeking out from one end. *Damn.* There was a person under there, motionless. I halted in my tracks and stared at the image, sorrow washing over me. I wanted to see if the person under there was okay but immediately I thought, *What a silly question.* He was nowhere close to okay. I dropped some money into the cup and moved on, thinking, *That's somebody's son. That's somebody's brother. That's somebody's dad. That's somebody's old friend. Once upon a time, that was somebody's baby.* I was shaken but kept moving, and because I'm a so-called celebrity and I have means and I got lucky, soon I was seated in the dark, private comfort of an SUV, speeding safely into the night. I stared absently at my bag of leftovers, tasty free-range chicken and lots of it, and thought, *Damn, why didn't I leave the food for my fellow man under the blanket?* Then I thought, *Well, maybe he's a vegan.* I snickered to myself and thought, *That's a good bit, a homeless person who's vegetarian or vegan,* but really I was just trying to cover up my sorrow. I snickered a little more.

Now I'm thinking of Snickers.

It's not the first "bit" I've thought up or done about homeless people. Once, I did a joke about a guy passing me on the street and I'm eating and he says, "I haven't eaten in five days," and I say, "Well, you're not getting this." Then I say to the audience, "I didn't *say* it but I thought it." I did another joke about how I once went three hours without eating but that was because of a bad waiter.

Jokes are one way to keep the sorrow at bay. Because, let's be honest, there's no chance the sorrow won't return. Oh, it'll be back, don't worry. Like the line by Bogie at the end of *Casablanca*: "Maybe not today, maybe not tomorrow, but soon and for the rest of your life."

Sometimes the sorrow doesn't even wait until tomorrow to return.

I really should try to do something to help the homeless, Mom, because it would help an individual, it would help my sorrow, and also it's what you would do.

Of course, it's no rare thing to see a homeless person in America. We see them all the time. Or, at least, they're *there* all the time. I'm not sure that most of us see them after a while. And getting to that point of being homeless can really, truly happen to anyone. We're all of us sad and confused at so many points in our lives. So many of us have addictions and weaknesses, usually more than one. (How do people *not* have a major addiction or weakness in this world? How is that possible?) It doesn't take much to lose your way. It's surprisingly easy. The stories are always harrowing and unbelievable—then all of a sudden believable.

Yeah, I suppose I could see that happening.

Yeah, I could definitely see that happening.

Yeah, I could see that happening to someone I love.

Yeah, I could see that happening to me.

It happened to me.

A week ago I passed a strip mall and saw a man outside a 7-Eleven and I thought maybe he was going through a garbage bin but I wasn't sure. It was twilight and hard to see. Isn't twilight the most heartbreaking time to see a homeless person, and think about the night that's beginning for them? Isn't twilight the most heartbreaking time to see *any*thing? So at first I couldn't see if he was recycling or looking for food, and maybe he was mumbling to himself—

And then he crossed himself. And I realized his mumbling was him saying the Lord's Prayer. He was about to eat, and he was gathering the pieces that would make up a godly meal all around him, on the top of the trash bin. Some people don't have easy lives. They just don't.

I angled into a parking spot near him, got out of my car, and walked over and gave him some cash. There's another bit about the homeless that I used to do, about how when we give money to the homeless, we base it partly on how we think they'll spend it. (Wow, I do a lot of humor about homelessness. I guess it makes sense if you grow up in the projects and your father is often jobless and the lights and TV often get shut off because the electricity bill didn't get paid.) But who am I, who is anyone, to get judgmental when giving a homeless person money, because he or she might, you know, buy drugs or liquor with it? "Yeah" (went my old joke), "I didn't think he was going to use the money to open a 401(k)."

Or (went another joke), "maybe he'll buy crack with it because that way, for a few minutes, at least he won't *think* he's homeless."

A lot of us are conditional with our giving. We shouldn't be. Either give or don't give. Right, Mom? Who are we to judge? "Listen, I'm going to give you this twenty-dollar bill, but here's how I want you to allocate it . . ."

Screw you! I remember how we'd get our welfare support in the form of vouchers, not cash. So if we had to buy clothes, we'd pay with the vouchers. It's really belittling. Probably not intentionally so, but belittling nonetheless. As if, had they given my parents cash, hey, you never know what we might have done with it. That fifty-three dollars a month could really lead to something dangerous. We might have started a business on the side.

Not quite in twilight,
Louie

If There Are Cheeseheads
in Bucharest, Blame Me

Hey Mom,

Hello Louie,

How are you? I'm writing to ask you if you could help me with writing my bachelor's paper, because I chose a topic, "thematic variation in *Life with Louie*, by Louie Anderson." I would like to ask you if you could tell me some useful details about the cartoon that nobody knows and some interesting aspects about you, because there's not much information on the Internet.

Your biggest fan,

Klaudia from Poland

Mom, many Americans know who I am (more older ones than younger ones), and lots of Midwesterners and especially Minnesotans know, but want to guess where I'm *really* popular?

Eastern Europe. That's because my animated TV series, *Life with Louie*, which first ran in America in the '90s, somehow became one of the most popular shows in Poland, Romania, and Turkey. So there's a mini-generation of people from there who grew up watching it and liking it and identifying with our family's life. The Andersons! Can you believe it? I based the show on my childhood experience, though I made changes. I moved the setting from Minnesota to Wisconsin, which meant the family were all big Green Bay Packers fans, not Minnesota Vikings fans. And while the dad was a war vet, like Dad, and his nickname was Andy, like Dad's, and he was gruff, he was nowhere near as angry and mean as Dad. I definitely tamed things down. That's TV for you.

Lots of details in the show are very similar. The title character, Louie Anderson, is chubby and funny and sweet, like me, most of the time. Louie has a kid brother, Tommy. And I gave them four older brothers and four older sisters, so that's close to accurate.

And the mom is Ora Anderson—kind, loving, and sweet-natured. Her character was voiced by Edie McClurg, a talented actress and comedian with the perfect Midwestern accent, who played the school secretary in *Ferris Bueller's Day Off*. Recently, while I was performing at a club, Edie was in the audience, and I pointed her out, and the audience went crazy. Mom, she's a cross between you and Mary, with beautiful red hair and a sweet smiling face and a voice that makes you want to eat pie. She could have fit right into our family.

Anyway, *Life with Louie* ran for three seasons and won a couple of Emmy Awards for Outstanding Performer in an Animated Series, and got nominated for a bunch more Emmys, but what I'm most proud of is it won the Humanitas Prize for Children's Animation each and every year it ran. The prize is given to "stories that affirm the dignity of the human person, probe the meaning of life, and enlighten the use of human freedom."

Okay, is that *really* what I'm most proud of? Or is it the *Life with Louie*–branded SpaghettiOs, in the shapes of various characters from the show?

Talk about making it! Mom, I would carefully eat each of the other characters, and push yours to the side, waiting to eat those all together.

(Do I have to add that little ° after SpaghettiOs in a letter to you, Mom?)

Now I have hundreds of thousands of Facebook fans from Central and Eastern Europe. (I know, what's Facebook? Remember the bulletin board at the laundromat, where people posted stuff like "Dryer #6 doesn't work!" and "Someone should clean the bathroom!" and "Judy's pregnant!" and "Watch *All in the Family* this Monday!" and "Who has an apartment for rent?" and "Anyone want a cat?" Facebook is like that, except with more judgment.)

My *Life with Louie* fans often post pictures of themselves in Packers jerseys or hats or waving Packers banners. And I always think, *Wow*, there's no way they'd be wearing a cheesehead in Romania except for me. My life, my childhood, the goofy, crazy Andersons of 1122 Hazelwood, Apartment A—we caused that.

I hope some of the other stuff I was trying to say with *Life with Louie* also got through.

Hi Louie,
    I grew up watching the *Life with Louie* series. Just loved the way your mother raised you and treated you the right way in

the toughest situations. Let me mention some of the stories I remember even now (after almost twenty years since the series aired in Romania) about her as I've seen them in the series:

- The story about her becoming a baseball coach for your team
- Mother's Day when she got sick and you took care of her
- When she won the award for cooking at the fair
- When she was against you working over the summer at the golf club and got more money than all the family had in a month
- When you got the first stand-up in your dining room after meeting the great Kazoo
- When you went camping with the classmates and she sent you extra underwear and cookies
- When she got herself a job of selling perfume and makeup for money when your father got fired
- When her mother died and you searched for a specific place that Grandma went because you forgot to thank her for all the winter blouses (the most emotional episode ever)
- When she prepared the Thanksgiving dinner for all the family and relatives. Your father had a fight with her brother. I hope that story had a happy ending.

I don't know if all these stories are true but I just love your mother for her mind, her soul, and her beauty in every way.

Best regards,

Mirela-Maria Iepure (Romania)

Anyway, sorry, fictionalized Wisconsinite Andersons, but: Go, Vikings!

Animatedly,

Louie

Who, Me?

Hey Mom,

    To be or not to be: that is *not* the question.

    No, the question is, Could you please get off your butt and pick up the remote control I dropped and slip it back into my hand, thank you?

    Okay, that's not the question, either.

    No, the question is: *Who?*

    Who is going to save me?

    Isn't that the question we ask ourselves, silently, all the time? Whether we're religious or not? *Who?*

    Everything else is minor by comparison. What's for dinner, where's the nearest gas station, when's my favorite TV show on.

    Nah. It's, Who will save me in life and who will comfort me and isn't it true that there isn't one person or actually there is, because it's really just me that has to decide that I'm enough, and that I can take care of myself and I can comfort myself. And that's why this morning, when I was at the coffeehouse and got my coffee (light, of course, you and I both put so much milk in our coffee, it's almost albino), I did *not* get the cookies, which came in six evil choices: peanut butter, chocolate chunk, peanut chunky, snickerdoodle, pumpkin chocolate chunky cheese, and plain old sugar. Are they trying to kill me? I was the one being confronted. It was up to me to save myself, no one else. I got out of there by the skin of my teeth. *Who* is what it's all about.

You gonna eat that, Louie?

Who, me?

Other people come in and out of our life but the real truth is that we have to find peace in ourselves when we look in the mirror, we have to come to the idea that that's enough, that we're enough, that we can survive, that we can be fearless and we can go forward and we can find our way, even when sometimes there doesn't seem to be a way to find.

In the end, the How doesn't matter that much, does it? If it works, it works. The Where doesn't matter, either, though it's fun to wonder about. (Will it happen as I lie in bed in my home? While traveling in another country? While sitting in a chair? While I'm at the state fair?) The What we know. So it's really Who, and When. And the Who is us, a new version of us.

So then it's really one question, but a different one from the start.

When will we be saved? Now? Later? Never?

Today's as good a time as any.

Saving myself,

Louie

I Am Christine

Hey Mom,

Playing Christine Baskets has helped me appreciate you in new ways, like the restraint and the optimism and the stress and the care you expressed or endured every day of our lives, every day of your marriage, every day of your life as mom of so many children. Christine is so aware of her faults and also of her strengths, and you were like that, too. I want to think I'm like that but maybe that's for others to say, not me.

Jonathan Krisel, our brilliant director, said about Christine, "You feel for her and the family she was dealt." Is that how you felt,

Mom? I wonder. It sounds as if that could be true of you, though you probably would never have put it that way.

When the show finally airs, I really think people are going to love the character. I hope people will relate to her because they will see in her their own mom or other moms they've been around.

Mothers are artists, in their way, wouldn't you say? They're like symphony conductors of entire lives. They're painters or sculptors. And not only is it really hard to shape clay into something really good, but that piece of clay is changing dramatically, all the time, even if you never touch it. A painting won't get painted if you just leave the canvas alone but a child will still develop into something even if you neglect it. Each mom and each dad has to adapt to what they're trying to make, hoping to make, and Mom and Dad also have to let that child turn into the creation he or she wants to be. Oh, and then lots and lots of moms and dads have to do this with two or three separate creations, simultaneously. Or, in the case of you, Ora Zella, *with eleven creations*. How is that not way more impressive than anything a great painter does? Picasso, Shmicasso.

Eleven masterpieces, Mom. That's what you made. You made them with love, care, and kindness. You gave them everything you had. You squeezed every ounce of paint out of your paint tube, used every bristle on your brush to make our lives more beautiful, more visual, you gave us depth, you gave us color. You gave us foreshadowing and texture. And, Mom, sometimes I think you didn't leave enough paint in the tube to complete the masterpiece that was you.

Jonathan also said of Christine, "Movies and TV aren't usually about that type of woman—someone who gained a lot of weight and had a family, and it didn't turn out that great." That's another reason people are going to fall in love with the character, I think—she's so real. She looks like so many people we all know. She's built like so many people we all know. And if people *don't* know a bunch of middle-aged or older women and moms who look like Christine and who are built like Christine, those people really need to look in the mirror and figure out what choices they've made in their lives to deprive themselves of that. They should head downtown to any city anywhere in America right now and just sit on a bench and open their eyes. They won't have to wait more than ten minutes before Christine walks by. Probably more like two minutes.

Here's Jonathan again: "There's so much annoying shit that people have to do just to get through the day—it's a struggle. You have to think, *Do I have my medicine? Do I have my stuff?* . . . People get excited about their cell phone plans, too—they get excited about getting a deal, and Christine is that kind of a person. She gets excited about deals, and she's got a garage full of stuff. Maybe it's an American thing."

Mom, you loved a deal. The 88 Cents Store. The 99 Cents Store. Two for ones. "Look at these, Louie, two for one! . . . *three* for one!" It didn't matter if it was crap. You loved anything that was marked down. Don't we all! If you could have found something that used to be seven hundred dollars and now it's a quarter, even though we didn't want it or need it . . . you would have been in heaven.

But you are. Never mind.

I love Christine. Maybe she is quintessentially American. I love that she can say, "I am in between sizes right now."

Mom, the show has amazing writers—but if I'm being completely honest, since I'm the one playing Christine and dressed up as her, every now and then, on set, often in the middle of shooting a scene, I will tell Jonathan or the writers what I think Christine should say and how I think she should react. And they let me. Because they know it's right. Jonathan and the writers don't mind—their ideas are there in every scene, so as long as we keep the basic content intact, it's fine. I just want to put a little bit more Ora Zella Prouty and Ora Zella Anderson and Louie P. Anderson and maybe even a little Louis W. Anderson in there, too, along with a helping of Mary and Rhea and Sheila and Shanna and Lisa Anderson.

You know what I wonder? When I think of you as I play Christine, which age and stage of you am I channeling? Is it you as an older woman, nearing the end of your life? You when I was just a little boy? You when I was a young man? You as I think you were before I was born? Are those yous very different?

I think I'm playing you as a whole. And think what an advantage I have. Not only am I sixty-two but you were seventy-seven when you died so that's 139 years of experience. Could I possibly have added that right? . . . Yes, I did. One hundred thirty-nine years to draw on.

I think people will respond to Christine because she represents a kind of reverse cool—she's so obviously her own person, doing things on her terms, whether it's bargain shopping at Costco or baking or housecleaning or trying to clean up the mess her sons keep making. I have also given Christine an energy, a feistiness, that I hope viewers will respond to. She's trying to take control of things. After all the heartache she's suffered, and at this point in her life, how can she possibly have the energy to do that? How is she not too exhausted by the very thought of that?

How? Because that's what *you* were like—that's how. Your humanity and empathy were big enough to form the sixth Great Lake.

The best thing about Christine's character, Mom? She gets to twirl. I don't mean twirl hair. I don't mean dance. I mean she gets to be alive.

The show premieres in late January. I have a bunch of *Baskets* media coming up. I'll write soon.

You live in me and with me every day,

Louie

My First Lady

Hey Mom,

It's me again. I'm not ready to discuss the day you left this crazy world. I don't know if I ever will. But I want to talk about the time I took you to the White House in 1986 to meet President Reagan and the First Lady. I still think about that experience now and then because it was a joyous event for me as an entertainer and a low point for me as a son.

We were there as part of an all-star salute commemorating the re-opening of Ford's Theater, where John Wilkes Booth shot and killed President Lincoln. That part of the festivities was bittersweet, too—the renovation was beautiful but in the museum in the downstairs of the theater, there were all sorts of artifacts of the tragedy, including the actual bloody sheets, more than a century old, from Abraham Lincoln's dying body.

The entertainment was Lance Burton, Victor Borge, Joel Grey, Freddie Roman, Jaclyn Smith, Tommy Tune, and me. It was going to be a TV special—taped, not live. We all performed for the President and First Lady, then went to the White House to meet them—Ron and Nancy! (Christine Baskets is a huge Ronald Reagan fan.) Not bad for a kid from the St. Paul projects, right?

Mom, I'm writing this letter about a very specific occasion that happened three decades ago because I was not a very good son that night. I was mean to you. Yes, mean. Yes, me. I thought what you were wearing wasn't up to White House standards. But my opinion was a bunch of crap. It wasn't true. Want to know the sad thing? The dress you wore was just like one that Christine wears. A sundress, in fact quite a beautiful one. It was absolutely up to standards. I was being a jerk. Why? I don't know. I still think about my mean-spirited, childish behavior that night.

Why would I be cruel? Because someone was cruel to me. And when someone is cruel to you, the cruelty has to go somewhere. If the cruelty happens to you when you're a child, a developing person, the cruelty gets in there, does all kinds of damage like a ricocheting bullet, keeps ricocheting around in there, and if you don't deal with it, if it isn't addressed and resolved, if you can't figure out why the cruel person is being that way to you, it will cause lingering resentment that just keeps ricocheting. So, Mom, that resentment came from someplace deep inside me, and I'm sorry that it got out, because you didn't deserve that ricochet hurting you.

I wish I had a less disappointing explanation for my actions. But even with an explanation, I still wonder why I would ever hurt you, the sweetest person I've ever known, the best mother ever. I can't undo how I acted then. I can only say I'm so sorry for being cruel to you, for the stupidity and carelessness of it. To this day it breaks my heart because I'm sure it broke yours. The best thing is, I know deep in my heart that you forgave me. If you could forgive Dad, then you could do it with me, for that.

Mom, I had the bullet removed, finally. That resentment of Dad. That resentment is gone.

And I know I've done kind things for you. I know that. Jimmy told me that when you were a young mother, before I was born, you would say things like, "Someday I'm going to go to Europe, and I'm going to have this and I'm going to do that . . ." And he would say, "It's never gonna happen, Ma" (though he told me he felt really bad afterward that he dismissed your dreams like that). And with each kid you added, the chance of your doing even one of those things got smaller and smaller, then tiny, then looked like it disappeared altogether. And then, in the late 1980s, I took you to England. We had lunch in Paris. I bought you a nice car. I took you to the White House. And at least some of those experiences and possessions you had always wished for, happened. I'm glad I could do that.

Still, please accept my sincere apology for my senseless behavior. Mom, you were and always will be my First Lady.

Your regretful, careless, and occasionally even cruel tenth child, Louie

Louie and Tommy

Thank You, Brother

Hey Tommy,

Thanks for helping Shanna & for all you do for me & everyone in our family. What you did for Mom, Billy & Sheila. Thanks for thinking about me. I can't wait to see you when I'm back in town for New Year's Eve & also when you visit me again. Life is short & we should cherish each other all the time &, like you, be willing to help!

Miss & love you, Truth Ranger, a.k.a. my Brother Thomas Todd Anderson!

Love,

Brother Louie

Truth Ranger

Hey Mom,

I've been texting a lot with Tommy, since we live far apart. I love texting because it's a great way to send a really quick message to someone, which they'll usually see pretty quickly, if not immediately. It doesn't take the time of a phone call and doesn't demand the other person be available when you send the message. It has an intimacy. I love that Tommy and I can communicate in this way, especially since I'm in Las Vegas or Los Angeles or traveling and he's in Newport, just a few miles down the Mississippi from where we grew up in east St. Paul, and it's too rare we get a chance to be in the same place together. But I try. We try. I loved and love all my sisters and other brothers—but Tommy and I are two years apart. He's been my best buddy, the sibling I'm closest to. The baby of the family. Number eleven of eleven. He and I were two peas in a pod, as Laurel and Hardy used to say. You know all this, Mom. He's funny, and he loves to tinker, and he's impatient, and he rolls his own cigarettes, and he's a hoarder (like us), and so generous, and really smart and such a good friend and he's bipolar and a little paranoid, and I used to "tiny talk" at him when I was mad at him because he was the only sibling who was younger than I was and who I could sort of bully, and later I made that part of one of my routines. He will always be my baby brother. I have given him at least two hundred tiny bottles of shampoo that I have taken from hotel rooms. He was so sweet and good to move back to the Twin Cities to help with our sisters.

The last couple years Tommy's been signing most of his texts to me with "Truth Ranger." He came up with an idea for a children's show called "Truth Rangers," which would encourage kids to always tell the truth. There'd be some adventure and the outcome would be a lesson about truth or lying or just life. He always puts the phrase in quotation marks, though he's used it so often by this point, he could just drop them. No one's gonna sue.

He'll text me anything—that's what texting does for you, Mom. Anything and everything seems worth sharing. A few examples from Tommy to me:

Stay away from the dollar store, you won't be able to stop yourself. Haha!

My neighbor Kelly knocked over the computer monitor/TV which was held up by a gallon of black enamel paint!

Have to perform brain surgery on myself! Just need one more mirror!
-"Truth Ranger"

I think it's the little things at least as much as the big things, maybe even more than the big things, that remind me to be present and grateful. I love having a younger brother.

Love,

Lucky Older Brother Louie

(a.k.a. Truth Ranger's sidekick)

New Year's Eve! (Minus the Booze)

Dad and Mom

Hey Mom,

Tonight is New Year's Eve 2015, almost 2016, and for each of the last twenty-five years I've hosted a special kind of New Year's Eve bash. Now, we do it at the Ames Center in Burnsville; before that, it was at Northrop Auditorium on the University of Minnesota campus.

So what makes it special? Starting the year after you died, I decided to begin each New Year honoring you. How? By having no alcohol served at the venue where I perform, because we grew up with a father who was always drunk and who made us live in fear of his drunken behavior. And of all of us, you had to deal with it most of all. So I wanted one night, in fact the night most associated with alcohol consumption, when people who do not want liquor in their lives could go someplace, have a great celebration, and not worry about drinking or being around people who are drunk. The Minnesotans and tourists who come seem to really love it. My goal tonight, like every time I perform but especially tonight, is to make people feel as if they're going to pee from laughing so hard. *There you go . . . let it go . . .* I don't want a dry pair of pants in the house.

On a dry but really, really cold, good Minnesota night.

The truth is, Mom, I wish we could have gotten away from Dad, the raging alcoholic. I wish we were strong enough. I wish you were strong enough. Can I say that? Is that another way of calling you weak? I don't mean that. And what would we have done, anyway—live year-round on welfare? Obviously you had something you needed to complete with Dad, something you felt you just couldn't give up. What was it, though? For one reason or another you thought that, in the end, we were better with him than without. I'll never really know. I understand that you had all these kids, and you must have told yourself, *Well, at least I know what I have with him,* and maybe you told yourself that there *are* worse men out there, and maybe you would have ended up with that man, or no one. I understand that it would have been a very hard road to leave him, if you had actually seriously considered it—there weren't shelters then, places to hide out, to go for support, to leave the kids for a while, as much as there are today. (Though there should be even more of those today, and better support and services.) I understand how hard it would have been because once you're on a well-worn path, it's "easier" to keep treading on it. (I put "easier" in quotation marks because it's a lie, Mom, it *isn't* easier.) But that path you're staying on, that we stayed on—we knew for certain it had monsters on it. We had seen them. We would see them again. They were always just about to jump out. And if the alcoholism "changed," as it did with Dad, and it no longer ignited into violence, well, it morphed into something else later on, a simmering meanness that was often worse than an outburst, because with an outburst you at least knew it would be over quickly, and you'd get a reprieve from the pain. (That's a lie, too.)

To this day, Mom, I still think about the drunken abuse Dad doled out to you. Hitting you, calling you a whore. There's a helplessness we all felt. Maybe you stayed with him because you loved him and you knew that if you worked really hard or prayed enough or loved him enough, that he'd be able to turn it around. *I'll stick it out and do the best I can, keep moving forward and maybe something good will come around the corner.* You were the most optimistic person or the most stubborn or the most determined, maybe all three. You "won" in the end because he quit drinking—but he never really changed. And then he got sick, and physical health or the lack of it is the great equalizer, and when a loved one gets sick, everything else takes a back seat and looks meaningless by comparison. Then it's just about survival.

But why not emotional and psychological sickness? Why don't they stop us from what we're doing, so we can address that? Must it always be cancer before we press the PAUSE button?

I know, I know. More questions that can't ever really be answered. But I had to ask.

People talk about how drugs ruin lives, and they do. I'm not downplaying how terrible drugs can be. But marijuana's legal now, at least medical marijuana, in some states. I'm all for it. It makes more sense to legalize weed than alcohol. Let's legalize marijuana in all states, and not just for medical purposes.

Because we all need something to help us get through the pain. I get that's why people drink. Weed is a lot better. Then again, fans and friends used to come up to me after shows, wanting me to smoke pot with them, and I told them, "Do I look like I need another reason to be hungry?"

The fallout from alcohol use is far worse than from marijuana use. I don't have the statistics. I just know that alcoholism still affects my life, and Dad's been gone almost forty years. I know that when you grow up in an alcoholic family, it's kind of like an atom bomb or a hydrogen bomb or any of those bombs where no one gets out unscathed. You're affected at the time, and also as time goes on. Its effects seep into your life, affecting everything you do, from the friends you attract to the risks you take or don't take to the whole life you try to lead.

And how about drunk driving? You hardly if ever hear about someone smoking pot and then going out and recklessly killing someone because they fell asleep at the wheel because they veered off into the other lane. You know what a four-way stop in Minnesota looks like, with stoned, Midwestern-polite drivers? No one will go! *You go . . . I'm not going . . . You go . . . No,* you *go.* I know there are lots of drugs that if people were under their influence, it would be absolutely terrible for them to drive. But we know what drunk driving does so often, not just severely damaging or ending the life of the drinker but destroying other people's lives, strangers' lives. A disease like alcoholism permeates everything. It's like the poisonous chemical DDT that was used to treat crops all over the country and the world that then caused people to have all kinds of different lymphomas and cancers—

Sorry about the digression, Mom. Back to New Year's Eve. I chose it because it's the one night in the year that Dad could justify his drinking and what a bunch of bullshit that is—"justifying" becoming a mean, violent prick! The one night when people have "permission" to beat their wives, or husbands, and abuse their kids, an alcoholic's dream. Do drug addicts have a night like that? Halloween maybe. I don't know.

As you know, Mom, my all-time number one addiction is food. It's my drug and a brutal one. What cartel brought Krispy Kremes into the country? Food addiction is epidemic in America because we produce so much processed food, fast food, horrible bad food . . . but also delicious healthy food. We have the best and the worst. I'm not sure when my food addiction started, Mom, but you must have known, right? That bread-and-butter combination is really what did me in, and led to so many other fattening foods, or foods in fattening portions. Yes: bread and butter were probably my gateway.

It's so fricking cold in Minnesota, Mom. I love coming back here for this show, and all the other times I come back during the year to see family, and to perform. It's not terrible tonight but sometimes it'll be, like, fourteen below, with thirty-six below wind chill or something insane like that and I need to make sure I have my whole tundra outfit when I come here. I get so bundled up that if I ever fell over, I'd never be able to get up by myself. When I'm bundled up like that and I smile, you can see only my eyes and my signature gap between my teeth.

I think that's another reason I do this special evening: So I don't have to go outside, from one celebration to another, alcohol or no.

I'm just glad that for the past two and a half decades I've hosted people on New Year's Eve so they could laugh their asses off. Laughter is the addiction everybody should have. Something that gives us great joy without any harm. It's my favorite addiction.

Happy New Year.

Your hungry-for-laughs son,

Louie

Domestic Violence National/Global Resources:
domesticshelters.org/national-global

Substance Abuse and Mental Health Services Administration:
samhsa.gov/find-help

The National Center on Addiction and Substance Abuse:
centeronaddiction.org/

12-Step Programs:
addictioncenter.com/treatment/12-step-programs/

– 2016 –

Yes Man

Hey Mom,

I had a gig over Valentine's Day at Horseshoe Bay Resort, near Austin, Texas, working with Martha Kelly, one of the co-stars of *Baskets*. She plays Martha Brooks. She's a great comedian and it was the first time we were working together like this, the first time I've worked anywhere since *Baskets* began airing, which is exciting. The place was interesting—I don't know if I should call it a rich people's resort but it certainly isn't a poor people's resort. Kind of like the Poconos of Texas. Or back home, Minnesotans with more money than we had would say they were "going to the lakes." A place where you have to save up a little to get away. At Horseshoe, it looked like the well-to-do and not-so-well-to-do came together for a wonderful weekend of golf, fun in the sun, and some entertainment.

But maybe it was richer than I first thought. As we drove by lots of houses with big sheds, I asked the driver why the sheds were so big, and he said they were private airplane hangars. Imagine being rich enough to have your own airplane hangar next to your house (or one of multiple houses, probably). Wow, Mom. I gotta work harder and make some more money.

Later, I had a really nice dinner with Roger's family and Nettie, who came up from Houston and Austin, and loved seeing everybody.

Then Martha and I met backstage, prepping for the show, and even though Martha was opening for me and I was the "headliner," I wanted to introduce her, something I learned from Joan Rivers, who was wonderful and generous that way. So while we were behind the curtain, and we could hear everyone in the banquet hall eating and talking over dessert, I took the microphone and said, "Welcome, everybody, and happy Valentine's Day!" We heard some cheers and applause. "I'm really excited about having this next comedian open for me tonight. I work with her on a little show called *Baskets*." As soon as I said that, we heard more people applauding and cheering! It was the first time I realized that people were actually watching the TV show. So exciting.

We had a great show, a ton of fun, Martha was fantastic, and we each went to bed and I got up the next morning to head home.

This week I'm doing a conversation on something called Reddit. I'll explain it later but I said yes because I've been saying yes a lot this year. In fact, when I got the role on *Baskets*, I made two promises to myself:

1. Don't complain.
2. Always say yes.

I've been able to stick to them, so far. I'm proud of myself for that.

Yes,
Louie

Podcasts and Home

Hey Mom,

Well, I just finished a Reddit AMA, which stands for Ask Me Anything. It was an interview with a lot of strangers, where different people ask me questions and I answer them on my computer, and everyone can read the exchange on their computer screen or their phone (yes, Mom, on their phone! But not like the ones we used when I was growing up), even though everyone is in their own home or office, or maybe even on the bus or at the beach. It was fun and the people were really engaged. What an interactive world it's become, Mom. In fact, I'm not even "writing" this letter: I'm talking into a microphone that's on my phone—yes, Mom, on my phone!—just talking into my phone, which doubles as a recording device (and a camera and a calendar and a calculator and a photo album and a jukebox and a place to shop and a place to make reservations and a place to play card games and other games, and a small TV set, and lots more). And can you believe that after I talk these words into my phone, it also transcribes what I say into written words? For the most part it gets the words right but technology is not perfect and now and then it misses. Like the word *words* in the last sentence got spelled as *warts*. Maybe I didn't pronounce it clearly enough. A small price to pay for the convenience. Once, *acknowledgment* was typed *egg knowledge meant*. You had so much egg knowledge, Mom. You made them great scrambled, sunny-side up, soft-boiled, hard-boiled, poached—you always loved poached. I think you enjoyed the challenge of making the perfect poached egg.

Anyway, it's a technology I appreciate. And I can talk a lot faster than I can type.

After Ratta I'm going towell.

Okay, I have no idea what I said there. But that's how the words got transcribed. Oh, well.

In a couple days I fly back to Minnesota to host a big shindig thrown by the Bloomington Convention & Visitors Bureau, this great evening where they give out awards to all these wonderful people who work in Bloomington's service industries, the best of the best of the area's hotel staffs. So they have "Bellman of the Year" and "Maid of the Year" and "Concierge of the Year" and "Front Desk Person of the Year." I'm sure I'll really enjoy hosting it. I think every day should start with an award and acknowledgment, maybe even egg knowledge meant. You should get applause when you come downstairs in the morning, just like an actor or singer or comedian comes out onstage or a great athlete comes out onto the field or the court or the ice. I think everybody should be treated wonderfully, and applauded, to recognize what they do and that they make people happy and make their lives easier. We need more of people—all people, not just the "stars" and the louder people—being treated special.

Earlier today I did the Marc Maron podcast. A podcast is a crazy thing, Mom—you would really love it. It's kind of an offshoot of a radio show that's CB radio plus ham radio, like where people used to talk to each other, and other people with CBs and ham radios could listen in, especially truckers and people who were good with electronics or who lived in the middle of nowhere and craved human contact. Only now you don't have to drive trucks or live in the Sandwich Islands to listen. (Ham radio, Sandwich Islands: okay, now I'm hungry.) You can wake up or go to sleep or exercise to people talking about cooking or murders or baseball or politics or arthritis or how they became a comedian. Marc is a very talented comic and a friend I worked with at the Comedy Store in Los Angeles in the '80s, when he and I were starting out. He was one of the first guys to understand how podcasts could really be used, and he devoted his to interviewing fellow comedians, and then his podcast got popular enough that he interviewed President Barack Obama, our first black president. (Yes, Mom, it didn't take as long for it to happen as everyone thought.)

Mom, I was thinking, I would like to do a podcast where it's me, Louie, planning to host a key figure from my life growing up, say a third-grade teacher or a dentist or a childhood friend, and in every installment of my show, the promised guest doesn't show up for some absolutely lame reason, and Dad—someone who can imitate Dad—always shows up right then, in my podcast studio, so he has to take their place, and he and I start discussing things, and of course it disintegrates into an argument, and he storms out, and the podcast ends every week with me saying, in a really super-annoyed, whiny voice, "All right, he's gone, see you all next week when my guest will be . . ."

Week after week.

Mom, the day after the awards event in Bloomington I'm having lunch with Tommy, Lisa, Jimmy, and whatever other Andersons want to show up whenever I'm in the Twin Cities. Then I head to Florida for a couple days' relaxation before I do a week at Off The Hook, a comedy club in Naples, Florida, which I really love.

I wish you were there to have lunch with us. We all do.

Love,

Louie

Tommy, Little Rhea, and Louie

That Was Your Baby, Mom

Hey Mom,

I have not written in many days. It's been too tough.

Last Saturday, I landed in Minneapolis, went right to the DoubleTree Hotel in Bloomington, and it was already five fifteen. I had to go on at eight thirty but I was exhausted. I snuck in a fifteen-minute . . . not really a nap but I lay very still and silent and recited some prayers and a mantra and took some deep breaths. My friend Jason Schommer, a talented comedian, came by the room and we laughed and had a good time and I talked about an idea for an animated series that I want him to take part in. We talked about life and all the things that come with being a comic. I said how I love being so busy and traveling and doing things that make people happy.

I got to the Bloomington Diamond Service Awards event around seven. The crowd was ready to honor some truly deserving people. The award winners were lovely, and I got to do a fun stand-up set. People seemed to really like it. Afterward in my room, I ate some room service, relaxed, and in my prayers that night I thanked God for all the people and good things in my life.

Sweet dreams—that's what I thought.

But you never know, Mom.

The next day, a car picked me up and we headed to Newport to pick up Tommy. Remember Newport, Mom? The old dump was there. It must have been on Native American land because I remember Dad negotiating with the Mdewakanton Sioux who lived near there so he could take "junk" out of the dump. People discarded stuff there and he always found things he could fix or use or make better. It was embarrassing and interesting at the same time. Dad taught me about the value of things without saying a word or knowing he was teaching me. So many things that seem broken or useless can actually be fixed. That's easy if it's mechanical or electronic or a piece of furniture. It's a lot harder when it's a person or a family.

Anyway, I picked up Tommy and he did not look good. I almost said something but I thought, *Well, maybe he didn't sleep much or he just had a bad night.* I did ask if he was okay, and he said he was fine. But Tommy the Truth Ranger was never one to tell the truth about how he was feeling, so I got into the habit long ago of not asking. Which was wrong. I should have pushed.

We went to Applebee's, not my first choice, but the rest of the group—including Jimmy and his new love, Lela, and David Anderson and his new wife, Melcar—was happy because everybody can find something they want there, and you can get two entrées + one appetizer for $20, which is one of Tommy's favorite things. He got shrimp and pasta, I think. He looked like he was really enjoying himself, and we all were, though Lisa couldn't make it because something came up with her. We had some good laughs and took pictures, then hung out a long time, maybe three or four hours. I'm glad we did. I was leaving that evening for Florida, so we wrapped it up. I had to be at the airport for a five thirty flight to

Tampa, and I told the driver first to drop Tommy off at his house. When we got there, Tommy said, "You want to come up and look at my neighbor's new fifty-inch 4K TV?"

I was just too tired. I asked him again if he was okay—you know me, Mom, I always want to know how everybody else is doing—and he said, "Yeah, I'm good." We hugged. I told him I loved him and he told me he loved me.

I headed to the airport, got to my hotel in Florida about nine thirty, and was asleep by ten. The next morning I hung out with my great friend Abraham and other friends from down there, and somehow, I really don't know how, we all decided to watch the latest *Teenage Mutant Ninja Turtles* movie. We muted our phones during the movie. Afterward, I forgot to look at my phone and didn't check it until I returned to the hotel lobby.

That's when I saw all the calls I'd missed.

I recognized some of them. A couple calls from Lisa. A call from Jimmy. A call from Shanna. And some I didn't recognize with Minnesota area codes.

Mom, you know the terrible dread you feel when you see missed calls from people trying to get hold of you? In your day, it would have been an upsettingly large number, a blinking red number of calls left on the answering machine. Dear God, it's overwhelming. Something had happened to somebody. I felt like fainting, as I filled with sorrow and dread and all the different terrible things you can actually feel at once. But mostly dread.

Oh, no.

No no no no no nonono.

No calls from Tommy.

Shit.

Oh, God. Please God, no.

I called Lisa.

She said, "It's Tommy."

That was it, Mom.

Tommy.

Oh, Mom.

I fell apart. I completely fell apart. It hurt me when Dad died. It destroyed me when you died. And when Kent and Rhea and Mary and Roger and Billy and Sheila died. And now my baby brother, Tommy. My little baby brother, Tommy. *Why didn't I take him to the hospital?* I was wailing in the lobby of the hotel. *Why would God do this? Oh, God.*

Thank God Abraham was with me. He said almost nothing. He understood. He knew Tommy. He loved Tommy. He knew what we meant to each other. I made it up to the hotel room somehow, with Abraham's help. Inside I writhed in pain, rolled from one side of the couch to the other, moved to the chair, moved to the corner leaning against the wall, knowing I would find no comfort there, either. Or anywhere.

We were supposed to be the last ones left—Louie and Tommy, Tommy and Louie—to tell the stories about all the others, he and I, grieve together, grow old together. He was my number one cheerleader, always rooting me on. He was so proud of me. He loved being my little brother. The Truth Ranger. He was the guy I'd worked so hard to get off the streets. Tommy was my shadow, my other half in life. We were the last two in the family, the two afterthoughts. He and I were almost more like grandchildren than children, and we suffered together the terror of Dad's rage, the beatings, we shared the same fear, the frightening cruelty from back then and throughout our childhood. We had a silent understanding between us.

Nobody had heard from him that day. His body was found early afternoon. Lisa went to his apartment. He was on the edge of the bed, on his back, his arm over his chest, like he had started to get up and then grabbed at his heart. A heart attack, probably.

I should have taken him to the hospital. I should have gone up to see the 4K TV. I was glad he had had the 2 for $20 at Applebee's.

It wasn't fair. It was life. I probably couldn't have stopped it.

Mom, *please* tell me he's with you and you are both okay.

Your brokenhearted son,

Louie

A Moment I Think I Wish I Hadn't Missed Followed by One I'm So Happy I Didn't

Hey Mom,

While Tommy's body lay at the Cremation Society of Minnesota, waiting to be turned to ashes, I was in a car to the Tampa Airport, to head back to Minneapolis. Though even if I had been in Minneapolis, I'm not sure I could have handled it.

At times in life there are no words, no thoughts. There is only loss and sorrow heavier than anything you've lifted and deeper than anything you've ever experienced. The only word I can think of for how it felt to me: *deafening*. It was as if everything else was pushed out by the loss and sorrow, so that I couldn't hear or feel anything else.

When the cremation was over, Justin—one of your grandsons, Jimmy's third son—called me, like I'd asked him to. By this time I was sitting on the plane, about to pull away from the gate. The flight attendant had asked me again to shut down my device but I only pretended to obey, then continued the conversation. My seatmate, rather than giving me the evil eye, seemed sympathetic. She could hear that I was having a genuinely important conversation, which was making me very emotional. Justin told me he had been there throughout the process with Tommy's body, saying, "I'm right here with you, buddy, I'm right here with you," until it was ashes. I could barely hold it together. Even though I wasn't thinking about my seatmate, in another part of my brain I was so appreciative for her understanding.

When the flight attendant passed our way again, she did not have an understanding expression.

I had to hang up if I didn't want to be one of "those people."

I felt drained. I was so sad about Tommy. So sad I wasn't there with him in those final moments. So sorry that Justin had to be there alone with him.

The plane began to taxi. I looked over at my seatmate. I could tell from her expression that she felt for me.

"I wish I could get a sign," I said to her, barely above a whisper. I was crying in front of a stranger and I didn't care. "I wish . . . I just wish I could get a sign from God that everything is okay. Something."

She nodded and faced the window.

The plane turned onto the runway—and as it did, Mom, I swear to you, the biggest, brightest field of sunlight poured through the window, blinding me and my seatmate.

She turned to me, her eyes wider than it looked like they should go. My eyes must have been just as wide.

A tremendous peace washed over me.

Oh, Tommy.

Louie

Life Is Funny

Hey Mom,

Now that the first season of *Baskets* has aired, fans of the show and of Christine have been communicating with me, sharing thoughts about what they see in her, and memories of their own moms, too. It's beautiful.

The show got picked up for a second season, which is great. But I received word the day after Tommy died, so I was in a fog.

I'm still in a fog.

I've lost so many siblings, Mom, too many. I can't believe it's seven sisters and brothers I've lost. What an awful number for that description. It was six and now it's seven.

You lost siblings, too, Mom. Your sister, Aunt Iona, died years after you did, but you lost Perry, who I got my middle name from. And there was Viroca, your sister you never knew. (How did she get that name? Another question I wish I had asked.) Viroca, who got pneumonia when she was a baby and died at one year old. Aunt Iona said she remembered Grandma Bertha sobbing and sobbing when the baby died.

So many tears are shed, Mom. When Uncle Perry went to visit Aunt Iona and Uncle Ike in South Dakota, he had a dog, and Iona wouldn't let pets in the house. So Shanna, who was a little girl then and living with them, of course wanted to see the dog. And she walked outside the house with Uncle Perry to his car, where he had to keep the dog, with the window almost closed, and she saw this little Chihuahua in the car. And Shanna says the dog was crying. Not just whimpering, like dogs do, but looking up at Shanna and Uncle Perry and shedding actual tears. "Just like a human," she said. "I never got over it."

Love,

Louie

Comedian? Movie Star?
Leader of the Free World?

Hey Mom,

I'm in the green room for *Live! With Kelly and Michael*, preparing to talk about *Baskets*.

I don't want to sound big-headed, Mom, but I always thought I could be a great actor. I dreamed I would win an Oscar some day, either for acting or directing. I dreamed I would be one of the very few performers to win an Oscar, Tony, Emmy, and Grammy. Well, I've won only one of those so far (the Emmys for *Life with Louie*), though I've won some other awards, too. A few years ago I was on this TV show called *Splash*, which was a really great experience for me because I got to face my fear of heights by jumping into a swimming pool from a ten-meter diving board, in front of lots of people live and millions more on TV. I couldn't turn back—I *could*, but if I did I'd have loads of shame, and video evidence of it for eternity. Yes, it was quite a splash, Mom, and I loved doing it—but besides giving me strength (and some exposure to a younger audience), after I did my splash on *Splash*, the United States Diving Association gave me an award of sorts, making me an honorary member of the U.S. Diving team. I guess when a 420-pound person jumps off a ten-meter diving board in front of a national TV audience, he should get something. The whole experience was a gift. I finally got a chance to climb the rope I never could in high school gym class. Not only climb, but climb to the top and leave my initials up there for all time.

Where was I? Right, winning awards. Maybe I always thought too much of myself. Before I wanted to be a comedian, I wanted to be a politician, but only president, nothing short of that.

Fortunately, I found stand-up comedy. You know I wasn't much of a student. For a while after high school I was employed by the St. Joe's Home for Children in Minneapolis, working with kids from troubled homes, and the experience taught me a great deal while at the same time it broke my heart, preparing me to be a better person someday. But I wanted to do comedy. I was lucky that it came so naturally. I was able to make people laugh just with silence, which is a gift. Of course you have to have lots of material, and I do, but if you can get people to laugh just by raising an eyebrow or barely twitching your mouth and being quiet . . . Jack Benny was the master. Anyway, I knew I had something because I would try to make people laugh and they would laugh. Then I would be serious—and people would still laugh. "I'm being serious!" I would say—and they would laugh even harder. "You guys!" Then I realized, *Oh, right, Louie, you come from a funny family, a funny, tragic, crazy family.* When you're in a situation with an alcoholic parent or anyone who is crueler than usual, there's humor there because you *have* to find humor there. Or you'll go crazy. Or kill yourself. Dad's knocked out from drinking? Fake-stab him in the chest. Yeah, you'll be in a ton of trouble if he wakes up while you're doing it, but it's funny to do this to someone who's caused you so much pain and especially to do it in front of your kid brother to make him laugh and, anyway, there's almost no chance the drunk is waking up. Or kneel behind your dad, or watch your brother kneel behind him, like you're fake-pushing him down the basement stairs. Or lock the front door as your dad goes out to start the car in the freezing cold so he can't get back in. Cruelty begets cruelty. Do you have to be a cruel person to make such jokes? No. You *do* need to understand cruelty, and possibly to have actually experienced it, so you can find the humor in it. I really believe, Mom, that human beings have a cruel streak. You see it with chimpanzees. Sometimes chimps just randomly turn on each other, or drive other chimps away, or beat up a chimp that looks beat-uppable. I guess deep down a lot of us are just bullies. Most of us handle it well. We've learned to repress that side of us. But when the opportunity arises for a weaker creature to be bullied, the less brave bullies in the group, the less evolved, less mature ones who can't manage our natural bullying tendencies, spring into action.

Chimps, humans—same thing.

Now and then in my act, I do jokes that touch on real darkness, but I have to be very careful or the crowd gets sad and concerned for me. So I go broad instead and joke, say, about killing the *whole* family. Or take this joke I came up with about hecklers. Once, after a heckler said his piece and I dealt with him, I said to the audience, "Wouldn't it be something if one night I came out and did my routine and I killed a heckler? It would change comedy. Next week, I do my show and a guy starts in with 'Louie, you suck—' and the guy next to him leans over and whispers, 'He killed a heckler last week.' That would change things, wouldn't it?"

How did I turn into a comedian?

Sometimes, I like to think I was some sort of "pod," the tenth child, the sadness and goofiness and fear and desire to make people smile and laugh all brewing in me at some optimum chemical rate, until it created me, Louie Anderson, stand-up comedian. So I went from dreaming about being president and helping people that way (and making them like and love me for that) to being a comedian and helping people *that* way (and making them like and love me for that). It was a no-brainer because being funny was easy for me.

Then I made either my greatest discovery or my biggest blunder. I created a fat character and started writing jokes about being fat.

It made me very successful. But it also put me in a corner, a place where it caused me great anxiety to lose weight. Because whenever ·I lost enough weight to notice, people would say to me the cruelest thing they could possibly say, though they didn't realize it. "Why would you want to get skinny? You won't be funny anymore!" It ticked me off. They thought I was funny *because* I was fat. Maybe that's all I am, to some people: a fat comic. I just knew that if *I* believed that, I'd be dead by now. I believe I'm a comic who happens to be fat.

People don't like to see other people change. It's jarring. It's a threat to their own inability to change. Richard Pryor quit drinking and drugs and suddenly people didn't think he was funny anymore. Richard was funny till the day he died. It's just that some of his fans didn't want him to exorcise the demons that for so many years had animated his comedy and intelligence, and their memory of him. They liked *that* Richard Pryor.

"Louie, where are the fat jokes we love?!"

I assumed a character that is mostly sweetness and niceness— not the worst character in the world for me to play, Mom, but it didn't give people enough, and it didn't give me enough. You need some sides with your entrée. You need horseradish on your roast beef. Who wants to see sweet and nice with no loose cannon at the end of it? The thing that made Archie Bunker so popular was that he could say the most horrible thing—but he could also find redemption in himself. He could repent. He was more all of us.

I never knew how to be all of us until I put that dress on as Christine Baskets.

With Christine, I can be mean *and* nice, happy *and* sad. I can be everything in that character. I should have found that sort of character a lot earlier, and stuck to my guns that I could play and be someone who was not just Mr. Nice Fat Guy. (Mr. Fat Nice Guy? Are they two different people?)

But maybe, Mom, I wasn't ready for that next character until now. It's easy for me to blame the industry or the culture. But I have to take responsibility for my choices. No one twisted my arm to do the comedy and pursue the opportunities that I did. Yes, it's hard to stick to your guns in show business, but you just have to do it, before it gets too late. When you're a comedian, or even an actor, at some point you better know who you are. You better stick to who you really are and not try to sell anything else. Because if you do, it'll backfire. You won't be considered *anything*. And if there happen to be videos or recordings of you performing in a way that's not really you—and there will be—you'll die every time you have to watch it.

Is the message of this letter, To thine own self be true?

Not to knock Shakespeare but it's more than that.

To thine own self be everything you are. Be *everything* that's true about you.

The good thing, Mom, is that I may have saved my best for

last—or let's say my best for later. We serve dessert at the end of the meal because if we ate it first, none of the rest of the food would get eaten. This Christine Baskets character might be the beginning of a great new period for me. New kinds of roles.

Who knows? I might even play a man next.

Love,

Louie

Make Your Date

Hey Mom,

Happy Mother's Day!

Remember when you and I appeared on TV for that Mother's Day special, on *Twin Cities Live*, with other Twin Cities personalities and their moms? You were so nervous. I could see it. But you held it together and turned out to be the star, no question. Very funny and sassy. I was the butt of a lot of your jokes, a lot of fat jokes, and didn't mind one bit. Your timing was beautiful. Shanna was in the audience. She cried.

Anyway, today I did this Mother's Day event in Detroit, something I started doing a couple of Mother's Days ago. That's when my manager, Ahmos, asked me if I would perform at a benefit to help raise money for this program started by his sister Sonia, a maternal-fetal medicine doctor (an obstetrician specializing in high-risk pregnancies). It's called "Make Your Date," or as I like to call it, "Baby Momma." When I heard what they did, of course I said yes, partly because Ahmos's family has kind of adopted me, partly because it's such a good cause, partly because you had all those kids, Mom.

Make Your Date helps pregnant teens and young women in Detroit who don't have the means to get carfare for their regular appointments at clinics and/or with OB-GYNs, it helps moms with resources like health insurance, home visits, and prenatal care, and it provides them with a plan to help manage doctors' appointments and other steps important to a healthy pregnancy, birth, and baby. Make Your Date gives these young moms-to-be classes to learn more about their pregnancy and health. So far the organization has helped more than six thousand young women. When you're pregnant and poor, and maybe feel even more stressed and crappy because the guy's not involved, it's way too easy for these girls and young women to not schedule regular checkups or miss them because they simply can't get time off from work or school or they lack the money to go. They might think it's not that important to "make the date" for these appointments. By missing them, and not finding out important things about the developing fetus and their own health, the young women increase the chance of a low-birth-weight delivery and deliver their babies pre-term, which is the leading cause of infant mortality. (Detroit has the nation's second-highest infant mortality rate, after Cleveland.) So this great organization steps in to make these mothers-to-be more aware and able to get the help they need, and most important, the support they lack. Support goes a long way in times of need.

Remember how much we used to get when we were on welfare, Mom? Fifty-three dollars a month. It just about paid for rent in the projects.

Mom, how could I not melt for an organization like Make Your Date? You were pregnant more than half your life, weren't you? Okay, not quite but it must have seemed that way for a couple decades there. That's one of the reasons I wanted to help, plus having five sisters of my own, all of whom gave birth. Each year that I do the benefit I think of you and how important it was for you to get to those appointments, yet how proud you were even when you didn't have enough gas money or bus money or *any* money. Being poor is a drag. I remember we got the help from welfare and then we weren't supposed to have a color TV, so when the welfare lady came by to check on us, we had to hide the Magnavox. What a terrible situation, being penalized for having things that Dad actually got at the dump and fixed himself. And if he made too much money at his job, we would lose all the benefits we received from Aid to Families with Dependent Children. Once you're poor, they really want to keep you poor. We should support poor people a lot more, Mom. Yeah, I know some people take advantage of welfare and food stamps. I know people take advantage of the government—especially really rich people. As usual, though, those who misuse the system cause a problem for those who don't. There's a whole big group of poor people who are so thankful and grateful for the help they get. I think about how you and Dad were so resourceful at cutting corners, cutting coupons, you even cutting our hair, Mom, that terrible bowl cut. Remember those times when we had just enough money to pay either the gas bill or the electric bill but not both, and you of course would pay the gas bill because we needed it for heating and cooking? So it was dark and you lit lots of candles, including all the church candles you stole. And, Mom, remember how we somehow had a Hanukkah menorah (you're such a pack rat, like me), which holds nine candles, and even though your family goes all the way back to the *Mayflower* and Dad's family is Scandinavian-Lutheran, you used the menorah to help light the house?

That was a *mitzvah*. You were always so resourceful, Mom, which poor people have to be so much more than those who aren't poor. Your kindness saved us—literally. We were poor, and there were so many of us, but because you were sweet and thoughtful, and so beloved by your friends, they helped us get through. Every few weeks, after Monny's husband left for work, you would go over to her place by the Hans Brewery, and she would open up her big freezer, and take out these big roasts and give them to you, for all of us. Monny had as big a heart as you. There's pride and then there's survival. You always knew what mattered.

I remember Halloween for the candy but also how all us kids from poorer families would go either as ghosts or bums because everyone at least had a sheet. Hopefully it was clean.

Anyway, Mom, helping with Make Your Date is about the best thing I can think to do on Mother's Day, and it helps all these young women and especially these babies, and one of those babies might one day save us all. That's what I always think: Who is going to save us? Is it going to be just one person? A bunch of people? I'm counting on it. I mean, I know we all have to save ourselves but . . . you get it. Someone to save us from all the other big scary stuff out there. I hope somebody comes along and says the right thing that sparks us to start getting along better, to start feeling more inclusive toward one another, to start being less divisive. We really need people to start reaching out. From church pew to church pew, neighbor to neighbor, make us realize that we're all in the same boat and it's sinking and no one seems to care and the people who aren't helping are the ones who aren't in the boat or they *think* they aren't but really they are, right along with the rest of us, and they're going down with all of us unless we all—*all*—take a hard look at who we are and what we're doing. I try to take that hard look but I also know I can be selfish at times. I need to work even more at being a nicer person, a more giving person. Make Your Date might just save lives. Healthier babies will be born into the world. Pretty fantastic. You saved our lives, Mom. I don't think you looked at it like that but you did. I have so many more questions for you, like, Did you give birth to any babies at home? I remember you said that when Kent was a baby, there was no crib, so he slept in the top drawer of the dresser. They're selling that concept again with these baby boxes. What goes around comes around, I guess, because so many of the old ideas were actually pretty smart. History matters. It matters if we're going to make the best of things in our own individual lives, in America, in the world. What are we doing to our world? God, I sound like a preacher or a blowhard. Mom, you always liked to call people "blowhards" when they were being, well, blowhards. Sorry about that. But I know you're proud of me for doing what I did today.

Hope I wasn't too hard of a birth!

Louie

Sweet Lisa

Hey Louie,

Mom was a very strong woman. She came from a well-to-do family and then she married Dad. She just loved him so much. They had nothing but she didn't care. THAT'S LOVE. She figured out how to get by. Her love and kindness melted your heart. Everyone loved her sweetness. She was always fun. Mom, I miss your love. And the sweet morning call up the stairs, "Lisa! Louie! Time to get up for school!!" She was never mean. I think about how great she was even though Dad made life hell for her. She was so strong. She was the best cook in the world, when we had food to eat. She made the best fried chicken in her cast-iron skillet. And the best angel food cake. Oh, I can't forget the best over-easy eggs ever. Yummy. Also, the Coke and tuna sandwich special with Mom—we would go to Woolworth's and have a chocolate Coke and tuna sandwich. It was such special Mom time. And she was always right. She would tell us don't do something or this will happen. And she was always right. I think she had psychic abilities. Remember when Mom started wearing pantsuits? We had to show her how to walk in them. She was adorable, how she held her legs tight together. If you saw it, it was so funny. She was a doll. Because of her I'm a better person. I saw her struggle so much with Dad's drinking, I knew I would never be like him. Don't get me wrong, I loved Dad. I just didn't like his drinking. I love Christine in *Baskets*. That IS Mom. She would love the show. She always wore dresses and loved to wear earrings and brooches. You're a doll, doing Mommy.

Love,

Lisa

Big Shot

Hey Mom,

Everyone wants to be a big shot in their family. I don't care who you are: when the main driving force in your career and your life is to become a "success," a big shot, you're really doing it so you can be a big shot in your family, with your brothers and sisters, with your mom and dad, with your friends and your girlfriend or boyfriend who you grew up with or who maybe ignored you. You want to be a big shot in your neighborhood, your community. Of course you do. You devote all that energy to becoming a big shot so that when you get back to town, back to the family home, back to your brothers and sisters, back to the family reunion, people say, as you pass, "He did well. He's a big shot."

The most important thing about being a big shot is not to act like one. Because then you're not a big shot.

You're a little shit.

Your son,

Louie

Andersons galore

Stranger Things

Hey Mom,

Recently I started waking up to the sight of moths and hummingbirds, big fat hummingbirds the size of parakeets, flitting around my bedside lamp even though it wasn't on, or spiders running up the wall really fast and disappearing. They never run toward me, always up and away, and they look back at me while they're running as if they've been found out. It's as if they're spying on me, checking on me. It's happened numerous times. They're not dreams. I don't know what they are. It's been three months since Tommy passed, and I've been wondering more and more about things like that, now that we've lost Kent and Rhea and Mary and Roger and Sheila and Billy and now Tommy, seven of the eleven of us. 7-Eleven, the convenience store. This is not convenient. 7-11 at the craps table. Whenever you go by it at the casino, you hear, "Come on, seven, come on, seven . . ." I'd rather have eleven than seven. Oh, Mom, that sounds so sad. I can never play craps again.

Just four of us are left—Jimmy, Shanna, Lisa, and me. Numbers five, six, nine, and ten, that's our order. The Final Four. The We-Dodged-a-Bullet-So-Far Four.

Anyway, I feel as if the moths and spiders and hummingbirds are there to send me love because that's what I feel from them, love, these big moths and plump hummingbirds. The birds are almost close enough to touch, and yesterday as I watched one of them, I said out loud, "This is not a hallucination, this is real," and right then the hummingbird darted behind the lamp, then darted back out and looked at me, then darted back, then I put out my hand and it came a little closer, and I reached out and it flew to the window and disappeared. Where did it go? Where do the spiders disappear to when they get high enough up the wall? Or the moths? Have they come to make contact? When the spiders and hummingbirds leave, it's usually through the wall or into some abyss, not out the window. Were they ever here? Were they hallucinations? Mom, are they a communication from you and Tommy and Kent and Rhea and Mary and Roger and Sheila and Billy? And even Dad? Actually, I wouldn't mind hearing from him, either. Maybe he's a spider.

It's not the first time something like this has happened. A month after Tommy died, I entered the bathroom of my hotel room, turned on the light, and suddenly there were colors, colors I had never seen before, moving around the bathroom. It felt like something trying to work itself out, and my mind immediately went to thoughts of Tommy, and also Sheila and Rhea and Billy. Those four. None of the others. I have no idea why.

"Who's here?" I said out loud.

I wasn't scared. It felt as if I could reach out to them but it also felt as if I couldn't get all the way there. I couldn't reach them but I could witness what was going on, and in a way participate in what was going on, and be comforted by them, in there, trying to work out what they were trying to work out. Maybe they were as sad about their having left as I was about their leaving.

It happened the next night, too. Same thing. Only this time I didn't worry about what had happened.

I lay down and fell asleep, deeply.

With love,

#10 (and #5, #6, and #9)

Stand-Up People

Hey Mom,

I'm in Washington, D.C., where earlier today we taped a tribute to Joan Rivers at the Kennedy Center. Melissa, Joan's daughter, called a couple months ago, asking me to participate. Given what Joan meant to me, of course I said yes. And thinking about the sudden passing of someone I so admired as a comedian and a person got me thinking of all the comedians who aren't around anymore, many of whom left suddenly or too early—Robin Williams, Sam Kinison, Phil Hartman, Chris Farley, Bill Hicks, John Belushi, Mitch Hedberg, Gilda Radner, Andy Kaufman, Patrice O'Neal, John Candy, Madeline Kahn, Bernie Mac—the list is too damn long, Mom! Not everyone is lucky enough to hang around like Bob Hope or George Burns, who both died at one hundred.

I think of the comedians who are gone, and who were so influential to me and my career. Henny Youngman, king of the one-liner and terrible violin playing, really liked me and gave me encouragement early on that I desperately needed. When he hosted the First Annual Comedy Competition in St. Louis, and I was disappointed to take third place, he handed me my trophy (a plastic banana) and whispered to me, "You were the best, you should've won." You can imagine how that feels to a young comedian. Later on, he hired me to write for him.

When Rodney Dangerfield came to town to play the Carlton Celebrity Room, all the young, aspiring Twin Cities comics were so excited to see him. I had read in an article that he liked Scotch, so I bought a bottle of Glenlivet and balloons, and presented them to him. He never forgot the gesture.

Then there's Joan. I first met her in Minneapolis, in the very early 1980s, way before I moved to Los Angeles. She saw my act and loved it. "You're a natural," she said. From then on we stayed in touch. She told people about me, opened doors. After I moved west and got on *The Tonight Show Starring Johnny Carson* and tasted some success, and Joan got her own talk show, I was the first comedian she asked to be on it. Lots of potential guests said no because they heard that Johnny was furious with her for starting her show and competing with him, and word spread that if you did Joan's show, you would be blacklisted from Johnny's. I said yes to Joan anyway and I'm glad I did. She was doing something monumental, a woman getting her own talk show. She had been good to me. And I liked and admired her. Oh, and I also did it because she picked me first. Growing up I was almost always the last kid picked for any team.

Joan was known as the hardest-working comedian in the business. She was a different kind of comedian from me—I told stories with jokes in them, more in the mold of Jonathan Winters, with some easy Jack Benny and Bob Hope pacing thrown in there, too—but I felt I could learn so much from watching how seriously she took what she did. And she had to do it even harder and better than that because of the misogyny in show business and comedy, especially back then. At that time, a woman was never considered equal in stand-up, no matter how funny. More than any other female comic—more than Phyllis Diller or Lucille Ball or Carol

Burnett or Lily Tomlin—Joan made possible the success of so many of today's great female comedians who regularly pack huge theaters or play Vegas or have cable comedy specials. Yet even today, if you read Twitter or other social media, it's incredible how brutally critics and anonymous commenters, almost always men, go after female comics. They do it in a way they never, ever do with male comics.

I was genuinely moved that I was asked to sit in and host Joan's show after her husband Edgar's tragic suicide.

I saw Joan in Vegas when she was seventy-six years old, on her knees, crawling around onstage at the Venetian, doing a bit, and I remember thinking, *I don't know that I could do that at her age. I don't know that I would even want to.* Here she was, twenty years older than me, on all fours, and I'm just trying to fit my fat butt into a seat. I always felt that Joan absolutely lived for the audience. I mean, that's true of all us comedians but it seemed to burn even brighter in her.

At the tribute, Gilbert Gottfried was there and Dick Cavett and Bob Saget and many others. We all told favorite Joan jokes. I recited Joan's line that "Elizabeth Taylor was so fat, a ship broke a bottle over her."

I think Joan's legacy in the comedy world is profound—as a trailblazer for women, and just an incredibly funny person.

I appreciate the greats, the history, what came before. One of my biggest regrets is declining an invitation years ago to be on a Bob Hope special. What the hell was I thinking? He was such a big influence on my joke telling, especially that timing of his. And now it's too late.

They're all gone, Mom. Not that I expected the old guard would be around forever. But we all get nostalgic. And it makes me think of how I fell in love with comedy and comedians to begin with. I remember watching *The Tonight Show* with Dad. I was such a big fan of Jack Benny's, and I loved the comedy of Jonathan Winters and Richard Pryor. And the late, great Jackie Vernon, who was sort of a sad sack. Which is what my character has often been. I used to do mostly one-liners, just fat jokes, so it was a fat character, very deliberate and efficient in the delivery, like Hope. You know I developed my skills at Mickey Finn's in Minneapolis, a tiny locals' bar on Third and Central. If you blinked, you walked right by it. That's where I grew up with other young comics like Jeff Gerbino, Alex Cole, Jeff Cesario, Scott Hansen, Joel Hodgson, Lizz Winstead, Bill Bauer. It was an exciting comedy and performance scene in Minneapolis, a city with more theater seats per capita than anywhere but New York. (That's what they say. I don't know that anyone has ever proved it.) Very sophisticated audiences, Mom, just like you. Who knew that you and Dad would pick a city to live in after Kansas City that was actually pretty ideal for comedy? Would I have ended up doing comedy if I had grown up in South Dakota? Twin Cities audiences give you a fair shot. Though if they don't think you're funny, they won't laugh.

Jimmie Walker was also a great supporter, and he got Mitzi Shore, owner of the Comedy Store in L.A., to watch my set in 1982. Then I got my big shot on *The Tonight Show* in 1984, and Johnny had me back a whole bunch of times over the next year. Eventually I got an agent who represented (among others) Bob Hope, Johnny Mathis, and Marlene Dietrich, and he started getting me gigs. As I got more notice, I opened for lots of huge music acts—Chuck Berry (my first words to him were "Hey, Chuck"; he quickly corrected me with "*MISSS*-ter Berry") and Crosby, Stills & Nash and the Commodores and the Pointer Sisters and Smokey Robinson and Natalie Cole and Glen Campbell and Ray Charles. This was mostly in Las Vegas, and I was doing well. When I ran into Joan around this time, I remember her saying, "Isn't the money good?" I was about to reply, "Oh, the money doesn't mean anything," but that would have been a lie.

There are things that come with being a comedian that I hadn't thought too much about, or liked very much. (That is, *besides* the occasional impossible task of having to follow onstage a young Robin Williams or a young Eddie Murphy or a young Sam Kinison.) There's also the choice of path to take, when you become successful. One path might be more lucrative, one more honest, though for some performers they might be one and the same path, I don't know. But those performers who are willing to say, basically, "I don't care if you like me or not—*this* is what I want to talk about": those are my comedy heroes. The ones who care more about being respected than liked. I was a poor kid who wanted to be liked, no matter what, and I wanted to have enough money to not worry about it. The money *was* good. The money *did* matter.

In the end, there's nothing more satisfying than when someone comes up to me and tells me that something I said resonated with them, some joke or routine, from twenty years ago, made them laugh so hard they nearly peed (good) or actually peed (better!), or even made them want to do stand-up. When I hear that, I smile. I'm glad I worked hard on that joke, that bit, that set.

Of course, comedy is a tough life. And let's face it, Mom, we're a pretty screwed-up bunch of people, comics are—sad sacks and volcanoes and damaged goods. A TV producer once said to me, "I didn't realize until I was working with so many comedians the level of self-loathing. Does any group hate themselves more?"

"Let me check and get back to you on that," I joked but I think she's right. Comedians are complicated people.

Mom, I don't hate myself, at least nowhere near the degree I used to. Still, I think it's a mean stew. You know how when you burn a stew or soup, even if it's edible, you can always still taste the part that burned, that bitter taste? That's us. That part never leaves. There's a helpless, debilitating place, so we need to make people laugh, so we can get all the love we can, and maybe enough laughs and love will cleanse us. Like a good body cleanse. Even a juice cleanse.

Who knows, though? Some people question the whole life that goes into it and whether it's worth it. After I got some national attention, the mom of an up-and-coming Minnesota comedian wrote me a letter, begging me to call her very funny, very talented son and convince him to not become a comic.

What was I supposed to do? Call him and say, "Don't follow your passion"? Call the mom and say, "Well, it's not the *worst* job in the world"?

I did neither. You have to figure it out for yourself.

Love,

Louie

Nominee

Hey Mom,

People have been talking for the last five or six months about how I'm going to win an Emmy for Best Supporting Actor in a Comedy because of my portrayal of Christine Baskets. It's nice to hear but way ahead of things. Anyway, this morning was when they announced the nominees, but I couldn't find it, not on TV, not on the Internet. I went to the Television Academy website and didn't find it there, either. So I started to doubt myself—until I got a ton of calls and texts and emails from my friend Abraham, my manager Ahmos, and my publicists Glenn and Eve Schwartz. I don't know if it was inside information or they just figured out how to track it down when I didn't. Maybe I was just too nervous. But there it was, finally, on the Emmy site, that I got one of the seven nominations for Best Supporting Actor in a Comedy.

Yessssss!

It feels wonderful, I can't lie. I read my name over and over, in slow motion. My competition I know well, from the comedy world or from their great work on TV—Andre Braugher from *Brooklyn Nine-Nine*, Ty Burrell from *Modern Family*, Tony Hale and Matt Walsh from *Veep*, Keegan-Michael Key from *Key and Peele*, and of course Tituss Burgess from *Incredible Kimmy Schmidt* or *Unstoppable Kimmy Schmidt* or *Irrepressible Kimmy Schmidt*. You'd like them all,

Mom, but you'd love Tituss because he sings and he's sweet and he has this way about him. Now I just have to wait two months until the night of the Emmys, September 18. Which means everyone will be saying congratulations for the next two months, which is way better than their saying, "You got robbed!" so that part's great. And if I'm being honest, which why wouldn't I be with you, Mom, I love that I worked really hard on the part of Christine. I'm making people feel a little differently with the character. I hope they laugh but I know they're also feeling lots of things because I am, too. If they weren't, and I wasn't, then why bother doing the show? With Christine Baskets I put myself in your position as a mother. I put myself in your position as a wife. I put myself in a position of a woman who has been through a lot, seen a lot, who feels everything, who tries to right all the wrongs in her life and in everyone else's lives, too. Who tries to take care of her children. All the things you did, Mom. And I keep one thing in mind during all the tough moments for the character in the show: Every time I have a turn where I must decide, *Should I be mad or happy or sad?* I think of you. I keep in mind your incredible humanity. Your depth. I'm telling you, Mom, you're really something. People think that I'm suddenly a great actor but I'm just playing you. I believe I have a lot of your qualities but I can't say that I'm the sole creator and author of this character. I would say it's you and me and we're in it together, and all my sisters and brothers and so many other people, even Dad. You have added the most, by a long shot—your wonderful outlook on things no matter how down and out you were, the ability to find a silver lining no matter how dark. I'm happy to play you, Mom, because I'm playing someone who is so real and loving and caring.

You're always just a nuance away, Mom,

Louie

You Gave Away a Child, or Two

Jimmy and Shanna celebrating their shared birthdays

Hey Mom,

Guess what I got in the mail today from Aunt Shirley? Some brooches that belonged to Aunt Iona. I'm going to pick out the best one and wear it to the Emmys next week. Iona had good taste, like you did. It runs in the family.

You were so good to your sister, Iona, and I've always had some questions about that, Mom, which I wish I had asked about in a deeper way when I could have. After you gave birth to Shanna, Child Number Six, exactly a year to the day after Child Number Five, Jimmy, was born, you must have felt overwhelmed. Kent, Rhea, Mary, Roger, Jimmy just a one-year-old—and now one more mouth to feed, more diapers to change. Dad drinking more, growing angrier, becoming more unreliable as a provider. And Iona had had a tubal pregnancy years before and couldn't have children. Let's face it, Mom, you were the champ of having children.

When Shanna was six months old, you gave her to your sister so that she would have a daughter.

I know Aunt Iona and Uncle Ike already had an adopted son, Bradley. Shanna went to live with them all in South Dakota, and really wasn't our sister anymore. She was and she wasn't. But you know that family photograph from around 1947, where Shanna's about four years old and they came to visit, and all the Anderson kids are lined up against a brick wall (everyone but Lisa, me, and Tommy, who didn't exist yet), and little Shanna's all the way at the end, crying? It looks like she's wondering, *Who are all these strangers?*

Mom, how were you able to do that? Was it your idea to give Shanna away? Was it Dad's? There are so many parts to the story that I still don't get. Okay, I do and I don't. I know that Iona and Ike were well-off, and we were poor, and I don't doubt you thought you were giving Shanna a better life and also making it a little easier on you and Dad and us. Who doesn't occasionally think of magical ways to make life easier, especially parenting? Then again, you did have another five children after that. Did you ever consider asking for Shanna back? Like, she was more of a rental? I know that Mary had been shipped out to live with them years before but then came back because Bradley and she were fighting terribly, or I probably should say that Bradley was fighting with her, because Mary was unhappy to come back to live with us because she liked her situation there (except for the fighting part). How many kids of yours did you think Aunt Iona needed to feel complete? When you and Dad sent Shanna to live with them, was she just the unlucky one because five kids were tough but six were too many? Or was she the lucky one? Did it have to be a girl?

I know Shanna would visit us during summers and even spent a couple years with us when she was going to school in Minnesota, but she considered Aunt Iona her mommy and Uncle Ike her daddy. Did that ever bother you? Did you ever regret it? Even a little? Shanna told me that when she lived with Iona and Ike, she had it good. She had everything. She had darling clothes and homemade pinafores from Grandma Bertha and the trim of her bedspread and pillowcases was crocheted, and she had all the school supplies she needed, which the rest of us Andersons didn't, and she had a privileged life compared to us. Compared to a lot of people then. She got to fly in Uncle Ike's very own airplane, a Piper Comanche, from South Dakota to the Midwestern cities he visited for his business, which was pinball machines and jukeboxes. Sometimes she got sicker than a dog flying in that plane with him piloting, and Uncle Ike brought those bright blue Dairy Queen cartons to keep in the cockpit in case Shanna threw up, but she still had an adventure unlike anything we poor Andersons had back in the projects of east St. Paul.

Which is another part of the story, maybe even the most important part, that I don't really understand, Mom. Shanna always stayed an Anderson, even though she was raised by Ike and Iona Peiarson, which no one ever spells right even if you tell them it has all the vowels but *u* (and sometimes *y*). She stayed an Anderson because you and Dad wouldn't let Iona and Ike adopt her, though they wanted to. You four grown-ups went for a drive once, and they asked you if they could adopt Shanna, who was very young then, and Dad wouldn't have it. And you went along with the decision.

I'm not even wondering now about what it's like to give away one of your kids like that. I'm not judging. Who am I to say what it was to be in your position, exactly then, with a raging drunk for a husband and partner, who was often out of work, and with so many young children. But here's the thing: Dad didn't like Uncle Ike! It might have been that Dad was a little jealous, because Uncle Ike was so successful and rich. Or because Dad was a veteran and Uncle Ike hadn't served, and Dad was so patriotic that he thought less of Ike because of it. Or because Dad himself was given up for adoption and never recovered from it.

But here's really, *really* the thing, Mom: Dad would pick on *Shanna* when she came to visit in Minnesota, because she was living with Ike and Iona, as if Shanna had made the decision at the age of six months to go do that.

Not letting them adopt Shanna really affected her. She got written out of Uncle Ike's will—technically, he left her one dollar—for reasons she still doesn't know. (Because she got divorced and they disapproved of that? Because they thought she spent too much money?) And she had no way to contest it because she was an Anderson, not a Peiarson. And maybe Dad was right not to like Uncle Ike—after all, the very last time that Shanna got beaten by her abusive husband, her arm all black from getting kicked, Uncle Ike never said a word to Shanna about it, never a "That's too bad" or an "I'm sorry," never said shit. And Aunt Iona would only say about Shanna's abusive husband, "He's a very hard worker and makes a very good living and you have a new house," and all that old stupid stuff that people believed in those days.

It just seems strange to give your child away to another couple, then have serious reservations about them. Or if you don't have serious reservations, then to not let them adopt and make everything easier.

Just another piece of evidence—what is that, Mom, like, eighty trillion?—that people are incredibly complicated.

So, yeah, Shanna enjoyed privilege when she was growing up but got shortchanged later. Her mom—I mean, Aunt Iona; Shanna called Aunt Iona "Mommy" and you "Mother"—left all sorts of glassware and antiques and labeled them with Shanna's name; Shanna told me that after Iona died, Bradley and Aunt Shirley had an estate auction and sold all that stuff without telling Shanna. And then when Bradley died, in his obituary it said that he was adopted, and Shanna felt bad for him, because it was the first time she could recall seeing that in an obituary, and she realized how much it must have weighed on him not to know who his biological parents were. Maybe being adopted by a good family *and* knowing who your birth parents are is the best of both worlds. Weird.

Anyway, Mom, Shanna's back in South Dakota, after a long time in Minnesota. She left South Dakota years ago because her ex-husband was stalking her. But he died in 1996, at age fifty-eight, when he went out on a wrecker call to pull a van out of a ditch, and it was thirty below wind chill and he just keeled over, a heart attack probably. It looked like he had broken three chains trying to get the van out of the ditch, and probably he got worked up and probably he got really mad, and probably he had drunk the night before, and when he drank, it was to get drunk. Anyway, with him gone, Shanna felt she could return home, the home she called home rather than the one she first came from. She adores her grandkids.

A lot changes, Mom, from the time we're babies until the time we're grown-ups. And eras change. But some things don't change.

It's got to be emotionally complicated, no matter when it happens or why, to give away a child or two, even if you still have a huge houseful of them, even if you're doing it to help out your sister who can't have them, even if you think you're giving at least one of your children a better life and doing the whole thing out of love. Seems a little eeny-meeny-miney.

Or was it just simple, knowing that your sister once said, "I always wished I could have kids and my sister had all them kids"?

Since you passed, we've all missed you terribly. But I have heard Shanna get emotional and say, "I miss her because I really didn't get to spend much time with her growing up." Maybe that's another kind of missing. I don't know.

Wondering about the differences
between Mom, Mommy, and Mother,
Louie

Midwesterners

Hey Mom,

How much do we Andersons keep bottled up that other families would have let out?

How much do Minnesotans and Midwesterners keep in, thanks to our famous emotional reserve (the nice way to put it) or repression (not so nice)?

There's a whole group of jokes called "Ole and Lena jokes"— you remember them, Mom, right?—about Ole and Lena, Swedes transplanted to America, specifically the Upper Midwest. I find them so Midwestern, capturing something very true of that sort of American, stoic and strong and accepting. Here's one:

Ole and Lena had been married fifty years when Ole died. Lena went to the office of the local newspaper to put in an obituary. She wrote something down on a piece of paper and handed it to the editor. It read, "Ole's dead."

"You know, you get five words free," said the editor.

Lena held out her hand, the editor gave her back the piece of paper, Lena wrote something more on it, then handed the paper back to the editor.

It read, "Ole's dead, boat for sale."

HEY MOM

If I had only five words for your obituary, Mom, they would be
Mom's gone, my heart's broken,
Louie

70% Disabled, Pending 100%

Hey Mom,

Remember, more than a year ago, when I did a meet and greet at the VA hospital in North Las Vegas, after that "silent comedy" performance I wrote to you about? I sat and spoke with many of the vets and took lots of pictures with them. They're each amazing and inspiring and beautiful, and wounded, in their own way. Why wouldn't they be wounded? We ask them to do things we're not willing to do ourselves. It's not a video game they're going into, where you can get killed over and over and come back fresh as new.

The vast majority of those I met were young men—boys, really—who served in Iraq and/or Afghanistan. But there were also some much older vets who had served in Vietnam. They're all locals, which is why they're at this VA hospital, why anyone is usually at their particular VA hospital. Not that I have to tell you, Mom, about veterans.

In the end, I sat longest with one young man, Tim, an army tank sergeant who got blown up and whose stomach and leg were all messed up. When you looked at him, you couldn't see his wounds but you could feel his pain. We bonded. Tim said they weren't do-ing anything for him there. His eyes were pleading. I didn't know how I could help but I told him I would make some calls. I had met someone high up at the USO. I could try Wounded Warriors.

I met Tim's mom, too. She told me that Tim had had lots of surgeries, with lots more to come. Her smile was the smile of a sad person.

Over the next several months, Tim and I developed a friendship by text. I made calls to the VA and the USO and Wounded Warriors, trying to help address the neglect Tim was complaining about. He was concerned he would be discharged from the hospital's medical unit prematurely, before they had "a solid plan of care and action" for his physical pain, and that he would be moved too quickly to the in-patient psychiatric unit for the mental health treatment he knew he also needed. Sometimes he apologized to me for texting so much but he wrote that he felt "out of options." He hoped I would be part of his "team" on his "journey to recovery." I told him I wanted that, too.

When I could, I distracted him with talk of new comedy material I was developing. He told me he was so excited to see it when it was ready. I think he appreciated hearing about the nuts and bolts of what I was up to professionally.

Once, he wrote that he'd been handcuffed and removed from his room because he had refused to go to the psych ward until his pain was managed correctly. Fortunately, another doctor intervened and said Tim should be returned to his room. I didn't know why he wasn't getting the proper medical attention. For starters, he needed surgeries on his knee and foot. He got frustrated because a round of CT scans and X-rays had come back normal, yet he knew how much physical pain he was in. Still, they gave him a "clear to go."

Mom, how many of us have pain that doesn't show up on a scan or an X-ray? How many of us have been cleared to go when we weren't ready? And where ultimately was Tim cleared to go? Back home? Back into the world? Back to a different pain bed to lie in? Only doctors and nurses who themselves have served should be taking care of our veterans, I think, because how can a civilian know what Tim or other vets are feeling? My trauma is sometimes a stubbed toe. I don't mean to sound silly but I haven't had my stomach blown up or my legs blown off, I don't have a face full of shrapnel.

We should be very careful about what we ask people to do for us, especially our veterans. Because they aren't just our veterans. They're our neighbors, our friends. They're somebody's brother, sister, father, mother, son, daughter, husband, wife. They're somebody's baby.

On top of all his other difficulties, Tim was having trouble with his disability claim due to financial hardship. A social worker was trying to help him expedite the claim. But Tim grew frustrated and angry enough to want to file a lawsuit against the VA hospital for malpractice and mistreatment. "I feel like my country is failing me and I don't know what to do to get the help I need," he texted me.

At one point, when I thanked him for his sacrifice and courage, he wrote, "I can't speak for others, but at least for me that's why I served, and sacrificed so much. For the people of the United States, for you and your family. It makes me feel humble that you and others recognize that sacrifice and want to give back and help us when we're in our darkest days struggling to live."

I continued to share small, personal things with him now and then, like when I was coming down with a cold. I thought normalizing things day to day was good.

Throughout Tim's odyssey, his will was incredible. "I'm getting physically and mentally tougher each day this shit doesn't kill me!" he texted me. "I see a pain psychologist as well as my PTSD doc 2-3 times a month. I'm now in a pain clinic, and as of this week got my nerve blocking injections for my organ damage, back, knee and foot. I'm praying they just amputate it and let me recover with a prosthetic foot. It doesn't work from all the nerve damage and it's just so painful." He signed the text with his serial number and then "70% disabled, pending 100%."

Even when things were gray, his communication exuded optimism, and he showed concern for others. "Down 3 organs and my whole left leg is done for—other injuries but those are the worst. I'm alive and kicking brother, they can't keep me down forever. Hope your cold is going away!" Or "I'm still waiting patiently for my disability to finalize. My mother wanted me to tell you she said hi! I'm sorry for the loss of your brother, Louie. If there's anything I can do to help please let me know." Or "I surely need an attorney to take on the big guys. I'm going to make sure what happened to me NEVER happens to another veteran again!"

Mom, we try so hard to be strong but our reserves are not endless, and sometimes it's easier to be strong for others than for ourselves. Sometimes, exhaustion and misery can't just be slept off. You can't just sleep off the experience of war.

After not hearing from Tim for several months, I received this text from his mom:

Louie this is Tim's mother Renee. I'm contacting you to let you know that Timothy lost his battle with all his pain. I want to thank you for helping him a year ago when he reached out to you for help, that gave us another year with him and he got amazing mental help from all your help. He did not end his life from the mental part of everything, he simply just could not deal with the horrible pain he endured daily. I just want you to know that that visit made him feel like he was worth something and I will forever be thankful to you for that. Here is the picture of your visit with him that I put in his wall when we laid him to rest. His phone is getting shut off, if you ever feel like contacting me my number is xxx. Also a page was set up for him on Facebook #ourbravestbrothertim if you ever want to take a peek. Thank you again for giving me another precious year with my Timothy I will forever be thankful.

That's all for now, Mom.
Love,
Louie

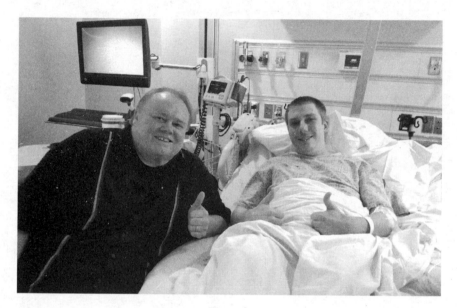

Timothy

Penguin Costume Time

Hey Mom,

Today I got the final fitting for the tuxedo I'll wear at the Emmys on Sunday night.

Beautiful tux, custom-made. It fits great!

Okay, a little perspective. When I tried it on a few days ago, the suit was too big in the shoulders, too loose in the legs, too big in the crotch and the butt. I just don't have enough junk in my trunk. But the incredibly talented costume designer Amanda Needham, the person who makes Christine Baskets look beautiful week after week, did a phenomenal job. I love what she does.

Then this evening, I attended the *Vanity Fair* pre-Emmy party. Mom, it's *the* party everyone wants to go to. They took a photo of me for the magazine. I met lots of great celebrities (I won't name-drop) who were all so nice to me. Everyone seems to like the part I play, which means they would really like you, Mom. I always give you credit. You're having a second life, and way more people could know about you Sunday night, when hopefully I'll be walking up those stairs to accept our statuette!

I'm going to bed. Sorry to write so brief but I can't stay up as late as I used to. You liked to go to bed early but you were restless. I could hear you getting up at night and watching TV downstairs, usually the local news or *The Tonight Show*. I know you liked it mostly for the background noise and the light it gives and the fake company it provides. So do I. When I was older and I would come home late, you would be up to say hi and give me that beautiful smile, and ask me, or me and Tommy, if we were hungry, and of course we always said yes because you would whip up your signature grilled cheese sandwich, which had too much cheese and even more butter, or maybe you'd make a sandwich from slices of pork roast that you had cooked earlier.

Now, when I get into bed, I follow some of your ritual. I like loose-fitting pajamas and a long-sleeve shirt. A lot of people seem to like sleeping in their underwear but not me—What if an earthquake hits and you have to go outside? I wear socks to bed, like you did, because I get cold feet, the real kind of cold feet, from the outside air or my own bad circulation, not the kind that makes people doubt what they're about to do is what they should do. I think Dad's feet were cold, too—hot temper, cold feet. And I always have a glass of ice water bedside, like you, with a napkin underneath so I don't hurt the table. And in case I have a heart attack, I keep an aspirin there that I can pop right in. Rosie O'Donnell says having an aspirin nearby once saved her life.

Anyway, I've got to get my sleep, Ma. Sunday I want to look as good as you did.

Keep your fingers crossed for me, Mom,

Louie

I Don't Have to Smile Like I'm Happy for Someone Else!

© FX

Hey Mom,

We did it!

That's the first thing I said when I got up onstage at the Microsoft Theater, after they announced "Louie Anderson" as the winner of the Best Supporting Actor in a Comedy Series.

Mom, we did it!

Then I said a few more things (after putting on my glasses).

I have not always been a very good man but I play one hell of a woman. This is for my Mom, Ora Zella Anderson, who I stole every nuance, shameful look, cruel look, loving look, passive-aggressive line from. I really thank her.

I said a bunch more things, thanking Dad and all my siblings, alive and not, and all their spouses (that's a long list to get through, Mom, before the awards show orchestra starts getting itchy to play you off stage—so there's a clear disadvantage to being from a family of eleven kids), and thanking Zach and Louis C.K. and Jonathan Krisel and of course Abraham and Ahmos and lots of people on the show and at the FX network, and many others. It sounds corny to say that we share these awards with others (and easy to say, since I get to take the trophy home all by myself, unless I want to chop it into pieces). And of all the people who share it with me, you're the one who allowed Christine Baskets to happen. You gave me something no one else did or ever could: life.

Winner, Winner, Chicken Dinner

(with mashed potatoes and gravy, of course),

Your son

Note to Thomas Wolfe:
You Never Actually Leave Home

Hey Mom,

We started shooting the second season of *Baskets* and on my way to the set early early this morning (5:30 a.m. call, which means in makeup and hair by then, and start shooting an hour or so later), still dark outside, I heard the sound of a passing train, which made me think of home in St. Paul. Is it Minnesota I'm thinking of, or childhood? I remember how, when I walked a few blocks from the projects to a certain nearby street (was it Ames Avenue or Ames Street?), I often heard that lonesome sound, a clear whistle, with purpose, a haunting, beautiful sound. To hear it was to be reminded that someone was passing through your town headed somewhere interesting. If you were ambitious and adventurous and really wanted to get out of St. Paul, the train was probably moving slowly enough that you could jump on. Or most kids could. I was too fat. And why would I ever leave your breakfasts, Mom? When I finally left St. Paul, it wasn't because I didn't like it, or even because it was, I don't know, six hundred below in winter. I left to find my future, my fame and fortune.

Whenever I hear that train sound, I get nostalgic. It's one of those sounds that takes you out of yourself, like a lone dog barking or children at recess in a schoolyard.

Not long ago I was back in St. Paul, on Minnesota Public Radio, and they introduced me, as often happens, as "Louie Anderson from Minneapolis," and I always correct them that I'm from St. Paul. But they'll forget and later in the conversation they'll refer to me as being from Minneapolis. St. Paul rarely gets any credit.

St Paul: the Other City. (True, not the greatest slogan.)

Either way, Mom, I have lots of fans from Minnesota and I think they like me partly because I'm so proud and clear about where I come from. The parents of Joe Mauer, the homegrown star of the Twins, once came to see my show and I was introduced to them afterward. Go, Twins! Then again, I have many Minnesota fans who, in typically direct fashion, tell me *exactly* how they feel. One man came up after a show, shook my hand, told me he was from Bemidji, and said, unsmiling, "*I* don't care for you but my wife does . . ."

Mom, can we ever really go back home?

After my appearance on MPR, I drove around the Other City, St. Paul, the place where you and Dad "landed," and I headed for our address, 1122 Hazelwood Street. A four-bedroom apartment duplex in the Roosevelt Housing Projects. You said ours was one of the first families to move in there, as if it was some badge of honor. As I approached, I drove by the corner of Selby and Dale, an area that was re-done a few years ago.

There it was. 1122 Hazelwood. Same as ever, mostly. 4-BEDROOM APARTMENTS were available, for some young family. Good luck.

Mom, you know the woods in front, where all the kids played and we had BB-gun fights? And any new development, which would destroy that play area, mysteriously burned down the moment it looked like something might finally be happening? Still nothing there, Mom, except memories.

Anyway, I looked at the buildings of downtown St. Paul. It's getting better. I can't say it's changed all that much, and some parts remain kind of run-down, a little dingy. Remember how we were all taught that the James-Younger Gang, made up of outlaws Jesse James and Frank James and Cole Younger and others, used to hide out in St. Paul, on the East Side, off Payne Avenue? The East Side was always Italian. It's a wonderful town, St. Paul, a real city, a workingman's city, but the streets do seem smaller than the streets of Minneapolis. Minneapolis is nicer and richer, but St. Paul has lots of nooks and crannies, and wherever there are nooks and crannies, there's room for people who don't fit in elsewhere. I see why it's the Other City.

But that's good. We need "other" cities and "other" places. Everyone needs a place to live. Everyone needs a chance. Because of the role in *Baskets* that Arby's plays (Christine Baskets seriously considers buying one of the local Arby's to run as a family business with sons Chip and Dale), I've been talking to some top people at Arby's about setting up a job-training program for young people so they can get jobs there and make some extra money and have better lives. And the Arby's people seem interested. Mom, remember our Arby's, the first fast-food drive-thru in the neighborhood? We loved driving through and getting the Arby's Junior, a great sandwich. You can still get the Arby's Junior Special, you know.

I remember driving with Dad on Tax Day down Seventh Street to the post office, mailing our taxes back to the government at the very last minute because the post office would be open until three in the morning. I remember driving in downtown St. Paul with Dad, and if I got really lucky, or Tommy was in the car too and we got really lucky, we would stop at the Coney Island place for a hot dog with the works—sauerkraut, raw onions, mustard, no ketchup—maybe two, if we were really, really lucky, and a Coke or root beer. Hey Mom, did you know they once named a hot dog after me at a place called Pink's in Las Vegas? (The original Pink's is in L.A.) A "Louie Anderson" was a hot dog with mustard, onion, and sauerkraut. Doesn't that sound delicious? Anyway, back to St. Paul, to when Tommy and I were kids and we might go with Dad to the KC Hall to play bingo even though Tommy and I were too young to be there, but no one ever said anything, and we played three cards for a dime, with no dabbers, and our markers were lima beans. And, Mom, when we got home and you found beans in Dad's pocket, you threw them at him, because he was gambling with what little money we had, even though it was just bingo.

Remember Jerry's Chicken, where they came to the car to take your order? And I remember the shopkeeper I bought red hots from. I remember the welfare store where we often got clothes, and Ames Elementary School, where they lined up "normal" kids on one side and us project kids on the other.

Seriously, who came up with that genius idea? Even then, more than a half-century ago, when the world was a different place and we're supposed to appreciate that people in previous eras behaved in different ways and we shouldn't automatically judge them as awful . . . Didn't *anyone* stop and say, "You know what? This seems like a pretty mean, stupid idea!"

No? No one?

Jeez,

Louie

My TV Family

Hey Mom,

I wanted to tell you about the people I work with. The *Baskets* crew and cast are extraordinary, so talented and so kind, and I'm beyond lucky to get to work with them. They're like a second family. I really love what I'm doing. Each day, I feel like a kid going to his own birthday party.

My dedicated assistant is Aida, a lovely woman who makes sure I always have what I need and get where I need. This morning she met me, as she so often does, with a hot cup of coffee, lots of powdered creamers, and a side of well-done crispy bacon, which I usually share with Hair and Makeup.

I got to work on time, as I always do, though I love to remind everyone around me, who gets there even earlier, "Look who's on time!" In the trailer, they put on my makeup, then my wig, then lipstick. All along, Martha Kelly was in the next chair, getting her makeup and hair done, and she and I started running lines. We had a lot of dialogue in the first scene we were filming.

Something in the makeup area smelled like potpourri, as if everyone's grandma had just walked into the trailer.

Martha and I had to stop doing lines for a moment because the sound of the blow-dryer drowned us out. But then we resumed.

It was a cute scene. We're good together. The mix of Christine's oversize personality and Martha's slight one makes a good contrast.

It was a very long day of shooting. I was in every scene and had very little downtime. I had one scene with an older actor who looks even older than I know he is. He reminded me of Dad when he was older, and also of Billy, though Billy was quieter, shyer. I tried to be as nurturing as I could with the actor, both as Christine and as Louie. It turned into an even more emotional scene for me because of who the actor made me think of. I was constantly on the verge of tears. God, I miss Billy.

But this is what I love so much about Jonathan, the director: he doesn't care how long it takes to get where he wants us to go. Yet he never yells about anything. He just says, "Yes, let's try another one . . ." He's basically saying, "When you stir the thing, stir it like this, maybe? A little more of that?" Again, I got emotional because of the way he wanted me to stir it. He knows how to tug on an actor.

He's not the only one I'm blessed to work with. Zach's a dream partner and a dream human being. He's genuinely interested in you, in any person he's talking to. (Me, I couldn't care less. I'm kidding, I'm kidding.) The crew is full of lovely and welcoming human beings. I try to get to know at least a little bit about all of them. Each of them has a story. Each of them has struggles, and such strength in dealing with those struggles to do great, professional work.

When I get to take a breather, and Zach and Martha do, too, and the crew is setting up the next shot, they have the "second team" stand in for each of us, background actors with name tags for the characters they're standing in for ("Christine Baskets," "Chip Baskets," "Martha Brooks"), and who look vaguely like those they're standing in for—like I said, it all feels like a second family, almost literally. When we're about to shoot a scene, and the aides yell "Quiet on the set!" and "Shhh-*shh*!" and everyone is doing their job and no one wants to mess anything up, it doesn't just feel like teamwork and a job well done but something more. We're bound by love. Love and kibitzing. "What color underwear do you think I have on today?" I ask a passing wardrobe person, before my first costume change. (She's wrong. It's striped.)

There are just so many people required to make a show, even a relatively modest cable show like ours, from the person who removes my wig at night to the people who serve the great food all day to the person who makes sure Christine is wearing the right necklace to the person who gives me the purse I need and the person who brings me a chair so I can sit while I'm waiting for the scene to shoot. It's like a family, Mom. When it's going right, it's really going right. (And when it's going bad, it's going bad.) Jonathan is the dad and Sally Sue Lander, the First Assistant Director, is the mom. Together, they provide structure and guidance. They make sure we all have one thing in mind, which is making something that means something to each of us. Zach's a huge star who could do anything he wants but he chose to help make a show whose message is ultimately about love, compassion, humanity. We can always use more of that.

Things don't always go in the order you expect. You film things out of sequence, to save time and money. (A crew member with a still camera will frequently pop into our break room to take a picture of us actors for "continuity" purposes, so that when we're filming at a different location a month from now, and Christine is supposed to have just gone from her house to Costco, I'm wearing the same dress and jewelry she was wearing a month before.) And in my career, I can say that things have not always gone in a straight line. Often you have to do one thing to find another. Sometimes you have to do a few things to find the thing you're meant to be doing.

Playing Christine is not just me doing an impression of Ora Zella. I'm trying to get at the essence of her, which means getting at the essence of you, and also the essence of me. I also think it expands to the Anderson clan. I think your daughters, as they grew up, were and still are all doing some version of you. And I'm trying to understand the very best and the worst of Christine. The heroic things she does and then the weaker things, like when she despairs enough, slips enough, that she retreats to her room to half lie on her bed, propped on one elbow, while eating gigantic spoonfuls of Cool Whip. I remember when Dad would be raging and you would retreat to the bedroom to watch TV. I'm just doing my best to play this woman as the realest person she is. The way she exhales with her whole body. Jimmy says Christine most reminds him of you when she's consoling her kids, when she's trying to cheer them up. But Shanna says Christine most reminds her of you when Christine is scolding or shaming her kids a bit. "That one look she used to get when she didn't like something, you capture it, Louie," says Shanna. She says just seeing me dress like a woman reminds her of you, period, even if Christine never said a thing.

I don't know how many people watch our beautiful little show. The ratings aren't great but who knows anymore how to measure a show's popularity, with DVRing and streaming (never mind, Mom—it's like a VHS, but better). I feel as if those who *do* watch it love it. Winning the Emmy helped, and if I can get nominated again and maybe win again, and if Zach can get nominated, which he absolutely deserves, then that might buy us more time, regardless of so-so ratings. I think our viewers love the show because they get the characters. Personally, I feel fortunate and relevant. Not that I felt irrelevant before this came along but it's exhilarating to be part of such an original, strange hybrid of a show. It's an adult family comedy. It's slapstick drama. It's got a lot of Charlie Chaplin's melancholy and hopefully a lot of his humor, too. It's *All in the Family* with more mental illness and work instability. It upsets people in a good way, a way that says we're part of the human race, and that most of our endeavors, even when we mean well, won't work out. It's about people who in real life would be thought of as dysfunctional, or partly dysfunctional, yet who still do their very best to function once in a blue moon.

And Christine gets to be the M.C., master of chaos.

My favorite line from *Baskets* might be, "I'm your mother. Do you know what that means? Does it mean anything to you?"

You mean something to me, Mom,

Louie

Big & Beautiful

Hey Mom,

Once, I had an idea for a line of men's shirts with the stains already on them—a little mustard on the chest, some spittle around the collar, sweat stains. "Life Shirts," I was going to call them.

I wasn't serious but I really *do* want to do a line of clothes for QVC or Home Shopping Network called Big & Beautiful, or Big Essentials, or maybe Ora Zella, featuring clothes that Christine Baskets has worn on the show or could wear or dreams about wearing. I model the clothes as Christine. She's the spokesperson, you're the inspiration, Mom.

What do you think?

I bet the phones wouldn't stop ringing.

I'm not saying that tens of millions of healthy-size women are watching *Baskets*. But the same thing that our viewers respond to would be true for people who've never even heard of the show. (Some people come up to me and say, "I love you in *Buckets*." I never correct them.)

After the pilot, when we got picked up for Season 1, I went through the wardrobe and helped the costume people select clothes. "My mom would wear this . . . My sisters would love that . . ." I tried them all on. If it was something you or the girls would wear, I picked it out. Really colorful clothes, lots of prints and floral.

Essentially, what a person who doesn't have a lot of money thinks is really fancy. Is that not a nice thing to say? I don't mean it that way. I see Christine as a real American, a big American woman, and that's how she dresses. I remember how soft your clothes were. I think your fashion sense was ahead of its time. You wore pantsuits. And I liked your appreciation when you had on the right thing. "I look so good in it," you sometimes said. Because you did.

I slowly disappear when I go into the makeup and hair trailer. (I'm not used to slowly disappearing, ever.) When the makeup and wig go on, I become Christine. And once I'm transformed, I see clothes as Christine would see them. The people who dress me, each of them has an incredible eye, whether it's for the caftans or the Easter bonnet or the jewelry. And I become more sure (and demanding? yes, demanding!) of my fashion wants and needs. *Give me some pockets! Wait, this is see-through! You'll see right through that!* I appreciate a great find, just like you did. *Don't you love a good bathrobe? Ooh, how about these pajamas? They're so Christine.* I understand about women lending jewelry to each other. Comparing outfits with other women on the show.

Whoa. "Other women." I have to remember I'm not a woman. I mean "comparing outfits with women." Full stop.

Sometimes I can get almost cranky about it. Once, I was given some great pajamas, big and comfy, and then somehow they got altered and suddenly they were too small, and there was no waistband, and the crotch was not right (do women talk like that?), it shouldn't go straight like that . . . but I told myself I wasn't going to complain. I didn't want to be a diva.

Christine Baskets as diva. Well, she has a little bit of that in her. And I think I have a little bit of that in me.

I see my transformation into Christine and think of what the great Divine did, or what Jeffrey Tambor has done in *Transparent*. Mom, I'm just trying to make myself completely disappear, and make you appear. More and more, when I'm turning into Christine, I look in the mirror and I can't take my eyes off of you, like the song says. And when I've seen clips of me, I see that I've completely disappeared in the part and—can I say this?—I'm sort of mesmerized.

I don't kid myself that I, Louie, am such a dreamboat, even though Ken on the show is clearly and believably attracted to Christine. I mean, in my wig, I look a bit like I'm with the Mormons. And I certainly perspire a lot in my makeup.

But sometimes you can't take your eyes off of her.

I wanted the editors to splice together clips of Christine, in slo-mo and wearing different outfits and busy at different activities, set to "Can't Take My Eyes Off You" by Frankie Valli. I used to open for Frankie in Vegas, such a great, sweet guy, and can he still sing. I thought I could convince him to do it for me. You know the clip would go viral. (A different application of "viral," Mom, but similar idea.)

Don't you think I should do a line of Christine's clothes? I truly think she's as legitimate a fashion icon as anyone out there.

In the meantime, Mom, they have a great leopard jacket for me this season.

Just call the number at the bottom of the screen. Operators are standing by . . .

Dressing smartly,
Louie

Older

Hey Mom,

I need a new knee.

I tweaked it on set today—not too bad but they gave me some ice for it. It happened in a scene with Zach, where we're sitting across from each other at the dining room table, and after it was over, I just stood up wrong. I joked with the crew that Zach kicked me, and you all saw it, right? Fact is, lately when I walk, the knee bothers me a little bit. There are twenty-one steps leading up to the front door of my house in Vegas. And a couple years ago, after working on a show, I slipped in the restaurant kitchen, on the greasy floor. I sued. They settled. But I need a new knee. The doctor told me this one's pretty much bone on bone, no cartilage, not even butter, maybe the other one, too. It's not surprising. These knees were made for a smaller model. They did not plan for this. I need ones made of titanium. Though first I need to lose at least fifty pounds so the rehab won't be so difficult. I need to avoid Craft Services. I've been pretty good about that, actually.

I could say all the bad things about getting old . . . er. First, we just try to hide it, as if it's not really happening to us, and to everyone, every second of every day. When I was fifty-eight years old, I liked to say that I just turned fifty, eight years ago. Well, now I'm sixty-three years old, Mom, so I just turned fifty, eight years ago, five years ago! I remember when you turned fifty, Mom, and Tommy and I just stared at you. What? Dad was fifty-one when I was born.

When you hit fifty, time moves faster. It does. And every body part starts clicking.

I try to focus on the good parts of aging. When you pass fifty, you say things like, "This is the best bowl of soup I've ever had in my life! *Can I have a gallon of soup to take home?*"

Why am I talking about what it's like to hit fifty when I'm in my sixties? Denial.

Then again, who wants to live forever? If you lived to one thousand, you wouldn't be able to retire until you were seven hundred.

When you're young, you do drugs that could kill you. When you get old, you just want drugs that can keep you alive.

Full circle, baby.

Mom, I don't know which is the most important thing about age: what age you are or how old or young you feel in relation to those around you. Do we feel old because we feel old? Or because everyone around us suddenly looks so young that, God, do you feel *old*. I feel so lucky to be working at age sixty-three, on a great TV show. I'm surrounded by twentysomethings and thirtysomethings and they still talk to me.

Sometimes I feel as if we're just way too focused on younger people (I doubt I ever would have argued that when I was one of them). I mean, there are millions and millions of people out there who are my age, who have money, and who want to buy things—but most of the movies and TV shows are not made for them.

It's trite to say but, at any age, we only want one thing, ever, just one: human connection. (And a decent cup of coffee.) Anyone who tells you otherwise doesn't get what's really behind whatever else

they're seeking—money, power, sex, bigger boobs, a nice Gustav
Stickley 1905 lunch table, whatever. I think of an old lady who
meant a lot to me when I was a young man. It was the first apartment building I lived in in Los Angeles, in North Hollywood, after
moving out there from Minneapolis. I knew I had to be in L.A.
if I wanted a real shot at making it in comedy and show business.
And I befriended a very old woman named Sylvia who lived in the
apartment next door to mine. I had just started to get a little bit of
success, and I had had my first appearance on *The Tonight Show*.
Sylvia had early-stage Alzheimer's, and very often when I would
leave my apartment to go to the elevator, or get off the elevator to
return to my apartment, Sylvia would hear me and open her door.

"Who are you?" she would ask.

"I'm Louie, your neighbor."

"Where have you been?"

"I was out working."

"Working where?"

"I'm in show business."

"My husband was in show business. The motion picture business."

"Really? I bet he was terrific."

"He was. Would you like to come in and I can show you scrap-
books? I have some hard candy."

It was the old ribbon candy, in the crinkly plastic that's twisted
at both ends, and even though they were wrapped, they still stuck
to the crystal glass bowl. They'd probably been there since the late
1700s. I should have resisted but, being a food addict, I would always
pry a piece or two free and think, *Jeez, for two hundred years old,
these candies aren't bad*. Sylvia would sit beside me on the couch,
then move a little forward, and point to the door of the bathroom.

Her live-in nurse often spent long stretches in there. Sylvia would whisper to me, "She's using all the hot water." Sylvia would never get around to showing me the scrapbook.

Each encounter of ours was a repeat of this, often verbatim, and I loved it. I mean, of course I felt for her—but what was I feeling? Sorrow? She seemed happy, at peace—something that I, and so, so many of us, have rarely known. Sylvia had yet to develop that constant look of fear worn by people who suffer from later-stage dementia or Alzheimer's, that scared-rabbit look—*Who am I? Who are you? Where am I? What are you doing here?*—and I never blew her off. I hugged her at the end of each visit. Did she remember those hugs, those visits? Did they mean something to her? She must have. They must have. When Sylvia died and her family came to dismantle the apartment, they knocked on my door to tell me how much my visits had meant to her, and by extension to them.

Hey Mom, I gotta go: one of the many twenty-year-olds I now work for is anxious to have me go over my lines.

Love,

Louie

Full Moon

Hey Mom,

It's a full moon tonight. And I think my acting today was the best it's been maybe . . . ever? Everyone on set felt it. Everyone was doing great work today, not just me—the other actors, the whole crew. It just felt aligned.

And I'm wondering: Could it be the full moon?

I'm not the first person to think that's true, and I believe in that kind of stuff—amazing energy permeating, for some reason, and maybe the reason is right in front of us, or maybe it's the white circle a quarter million miles above us.

I believe in karma. Good and bad. Bad is when Dad comes to see me perform comedy for the first time ever, at Mickey Finn's in Minneapolis, and the next morning has a stroke.

This morning, still dark, I woke up in a really positive state. Normally, I would have just lain in bed, summoning the energy. But I felt great, and I said my prayers, and I got up and shaved and everything was in tune.

Then, during the day of shooting, all these things that often happen—misplacing my bifocals and my phone charger and my headphones—they just *weren't* happening. Everything seemed clear, unified. Food tasted even better than usual. I didn't overeat. And we were all so productive.

And it turned out there was a full beautiful white disk beaming down on us.

Really, Louie? The moon? It's the moon that's causing all of this?

Hey Mom, have you ever heard the expression "waxing gibbous"? I just heard it. It means more than a half-moon but less than a full moon, and it's "waxing," or moving, toward a full moon. Why am I bringing it up now?

Just because I was talking about the moon. And I think it's a funny expression.

A little bit loony and a little bit lune-y,

Louie

Life Is a Performance, Old Chum

Hey Mom,

1122 Hazelwood was your theater, your children were your audience, and you were a great actress. The parts you played varied greatly, from young wife and mother to abused wife to fearless hen protecting her brood to confidante and great listener and advice giver and hope infuser to the many who needed that so they could go on. You played young, you played middle-aged, you played classy, proud, older mother of a headstrong young comedian who thought he knew it all. But you never wavered in your love for that boy and his many, many siblings, and somehow you had an equal amount left over for neighbors, friends, even complete strangers.

You could make anything or anyone seem interesting, even beautiful. I cherish the nuances I learned from you. You never left any of those who witnessed your life performances empty-handed or empty-hearted. And you always left your audience with a very full stomach!

Hold her up to the light and you see me and all her children, their children, and their children . . . in this way, she lives forever.

Love,

Louie

Seduce, Exploit, Abandon

Hey Mom,

I flew home from North Carolina, where I had performed several shows, which makes over fifty dates for the year, down from previous years but that's because I now have months where I'm filming *Baskets* plus a new game show. I love working and honestly it's not like work at all. I feel wonderfully blessed and so lucky to be able to make people laugh. It's the best feeling. You know that you could make people laugh, right? So I had one parent who could make me laugh and the other who could make me cry. (Dad could be funny, too.)

Anyway, when I landed at McCarran Airport and got off the plane, I did what I usually do—stop first in the men's bathroom between Gate 36 and Gate 32 because we're still so far from baggage claim. I have my favorite stall where I can regroup and get it together before I trudge through the airport, one of the busiest in the world.

But this time, when I got in the stall and closed the door, I saw this sign:

GET HELP
If you are a victim of human trafficking, call this number
1-888-373-7888
www.TraffickingResourceCenter.org

Is there anything more inhumane than human trafficking? What kind of world is this? I once watched a special on it and lots of times these victims don't even know they're in it until it's too late. Sometimes families sell their children to traffickers because they're so poor they need money. This is the end of the world for many of these victims. Or guys hang out in places like bus stations and malls, where they see young girls and boys, they don't care how young, and take them and sell them, and don't give a thought to what they're a part of. The sadness and terror and brutality of it. It's beyond belief, yet it's happening to a sickening degree.

"Seduce, exploit, abandon." That's the phrase my friend James Gitar uses to describe what our larger society does. It seduces us into doing things and buying things and consuming things and drinking things we don't really need or that are more bad for us than good. Then it exploits us by charging us more than we need to pay or can pay for these products and services (let's be honest, we know we're spending a lot more on so many consumer goods and other things than is truly necessary, because of status seeking, peer pressure, fear, etc.). Finally, when we're broke, and we lack the resources, looks, talent, youth, etc., society abandons us and moves on to a new round of suckers . . . to be seduced and exploited.

Capitalism at its finest! The Hollywood wheel!

The phrase "seduce, exploit, abandon" applies perfectly to human trafficking, too.

One of the saddest things about human trafficking is how many people must be involved to make it work. It can't be just one person. Usually it takes literally dozens of human beings to keep up the seduction and exploitation and abandonment of innocent young people, to set up these elaborate situations where this can happen.

What can we do to help, to make a difference, Mom? What should I do? Will it ever stop?

We should start by being honest with ourselves that it exists. I'm glad they put that sign on the bathroom stall door. I hope it's on doors in airports and bus stations and malls all over the place, and hopefully some people will be saved because of this awareness. In fact, Mom, I think the sign should be replaced with a button that you can push. You don't even have to make a call, which may be risky. Put these buttons all over the place. You never know who will see it or need it.

I pray for *all* the people who are involved in trafficking because to do it, you have to be really broken.

For those to whom it's being done, I feel so sorry and sad. We should put way more money into this effort because when we succeed, we are purely and simply saving lives, one by one.

To the people who are doing it: STOP.

Shaking my head in disbelief and sadness,

Louie

Human Trafficking Services for Survivors (U.S. Department of Justice):

ojjdp.gov/programs/human-trafficking-services.html

Blue Campaign: One Voice. One Mission. End Human Trafficking (U.S. Department of Homeland Security):

dhs.gov/blue-campaign/resources-available-victims

National Human Trafficking Hotline:

polarisproject.org/get-assistance/national-human-trafficking-hotline

– 2017 –

Jesus Calling

Hey Mom,

I need some faith to get through.

A psychic in Minnesota once told me I was Fatty Arbuckle reincarnated. Apparently Fatty came back through me so that I could right the wrong done to him.

Now, I don't know if that was just a psychic taking advantage of a physically big, fat guy just starting out in show business, a clever thing to say to build up that susceptible young guy's ego—okay, yeah, probably; after all, I gave her money for the reading—but somehow the general notion resonated with me. I've always been open to ideas, new ideas. Isn't it good to be open to new beliefs? Is it good to be open to the idea of reincarnation, that life is everlasting? It's a much better thought than that everything just goes black and we're done for. I gotta believe that. I've seen things and felt things and I want to believe that there are people from my life that have passed on from this world into the next. I want to believe in God. I want Him to show up and make everything better. I want so much to have faith but when such bad things happen out there it's really hard to keep the faith going. When people say that life started only two thousand years ago, we have rich scientific evidence to refute that. What I mostly get out of all this is that it's good to have faith. You're fortunate if you have it. Because faith helps people make it through the day. And if faith is what it takes to help people get through the day, as long as they're not harming anyone, or forcing it on anyone else, it's really no one's business. Your belief is your belief, whether you believe as a Muslim, a Jew, a Buddhist, a Hindu, a Christian, or anything else. Everyone should believe what they want. I just don't think we should encroach our beliefs onto others. Or judge others because their beliefs aren't ours.

I think you and I are on the same page with this stuff, Mom. We wanted and want to believe in a life after this one but only you know for sure now. I'd love for you to break into a phone call, and go, "Louie, it's your mom . . . ," and then I would completely blow off whoever I was talking to and I would talk to you forever, and see how it's going up there, or wherever you are, and I'd ask if there's anything I should be watching out for.

Every time I return home in mid-January (I leave Vegas from the end of December through the middle of January when the crowds are mostly underwhelming), I come back to lots of piled-up mail. Bills, junk mail, some interesting things—anyway, there was this one package that I opened and it was from Gayle, a very sweet, devoted fan of mine from the South who in the past has sent me letters and cards. Enclosed was a book titled *Jesus Calling* by Sarah Young, a devotional that has a passage for every day of the year starting on January 1. Gayle had inscribed the book, "Louie, May you live the one exceptional life only you were born to live. Love, Gayle."

It was January 16 when I opened the package but I started reading it from the first passage . . . and, Mom, it's a book I find comfort in. I have found myself reading the same passage for each particular day several times a day, because each time I read it I find something new. For instance, here's the very first passage, for January 1:

Come to me with a teachable spirit, eager to be changed. A close walk with Me is a life of continual newness. Do not cling to old ways as you step into a new year. Instead, seek My Face with an open mind, knowing that your journey with Me involves being transformed by the renewing of your mind. As you focus your thoughts on Me, be aware that I am fully attentive to you. I see you with a steady eye, because My attention span is infinite. I know and understand, completely; My thoughts embrace you in everlasting love. I also know the plans I have for you: plans to prosper you and not to harm you, plans to give you hope and a future. Give yourself fully to this adventure of increasing attentiveness to My Presence.

[Romans 12:2, Jeremiah 29:11]

The author of the book dedicates it to her mother, who "demonstrated her appreciation of my writing in poignant ways. She kept my manuscript beside her bed, so she could read it every morning. Once, while away from her home, she even asked me to fax her the readings day by day. After she died from cancer, I found portions of my writings that she had hand-copied into a journal . . . There is a sense in which she has written—through me—this book."

Sound like anyone you know, Mom?

We didn't do much religious stuff growing up. Dad would "pray" when he was mad—"Oh, Jesus! . . . Oh, Lord!"—or when he was trying to get back in your good graces because he had been such an a-hole after drinking. But we never really practiced any religion. We didn't have a family Bible. I went to confirmation class at the Lutheran church on Saturdays only because my friend Tony Johnson did, so I tagged along. I got a lot out of it, though, and some of it must have stuck with me. Is that why I've been reading this book every day? As I said, I get comfort from it. And I want to believe you're up there, you're with God, you're with someone, you're with my brothers and sisters, you're with Dad and he's turned out to be the nicer guy he could have become. Maybe we don't go up there as the individuals we were, maybe we're just souls who are comforted and waiting for re-entry . . . I don't know. Mom, do you believe in reincarnation? That's kind of a dumb question to be asking you but I want to ask it anyway.

Hey Mom, let me share the first lines in *Jesus Calling* for January 4, the day you died:

I want you to learn a new habit. Try saying, "I trust You, Jesus," in response to whatever happens to you. If there is time, think about who I am in all My Power and Glory; ponder also the depth and breadth of My love for you . . .

You feel how soothing this can be to me, down here? It helps give me faith. And I need faith to get through.

Love,
Louie

What Are We Waiting For?

Hey Mom,

You know how I wrote that the only real questions are *Who?* and sometimes *When?* I take that back. The big one is really *Why?* Why do we wait so long to take care of ourselves? Why did I wait until I was sixty-three years old to really start worrying about my weight? Why why why? I don't know the answer. I know I thought about it a million times before. But why am I only now starting to take it seriously? Why did Roger wait so long to quit smoking? He knew he was sick and that smoking had contributed to making him sick but he didn't seem to care. Why don't the Andersons seem to care? Some people take good care of themselves. They learn it from their moms and dads. Do I have some sort of weird default setting, where even if I *wanted* to take care of myself, I would default to not caring? I can't seem to take care of myself and now it puzzles me and it really bothers me. I know it's deep-seated because if I could change it easily of course I would. But I know I have to work very hard at it, and it has to be very concentrated for me to get anywhere with it. I know I shouldn't eat a sloppy joe. Just look at it. Look at all that grease. As I start to reach for the bun and ladle the meat on and close the bun on it, I'm thinking, *Why am I eating this?* Like I have no control over my hand or my brain. *Must have sloppy joe . . .* like I'm a zombie.

Why is it that when I'm trying to lose weight, if I weigh myself, it suddenly becomes so much harder? Recently, I was doing a good job of it, and eating better, and not weighing myself, and losing some weight . . . then I weighed myself. Bad move! Even though it proved I had done a pretty good job up to then, I was like, *Damn!* And, like that, it all got harder. Big mistake.

After you died, Mom, I got fatter. Then Rhea died and I got fatter. Mary died and I got fatter. Billy, Kent, then Roger, same thing. Then Sheila, which was a giant blow. Then Tommy, the caboose. I was thrown off the train when Tommy died. The train flew off the tracks.

It's so hard to change, even when that change is so good. I really wish I could change my inability to change.

Anyway, Mom, just wondering if you knew why that is.

At some point you have to park your past and put yellow caution tape around it so you don't keep going back to it. Because there's nothing like lounging around in your past and all that self-pity.

Love you,
Louie

I Miss Them All

Hey Mom,

I miss my brothers and sisters to different degrees, and sometimes that makes me feel bad, but it shouldn't because I was around them to different degrees. Some of them I was hardly around at all. But I loved them all and I miss them all. Kent, your firstborn, terrified me a little but I liked him a lot and I really miss his phone calls. He'd call and say, "What's going on?" Then he'd lecture me a little, because that was his role in the family, to get people straight, even if he couldn't always straighten himself out. Sometimes he picked locks and cracked safes, and he got caught doing that a couple times, but he got away with it a lot more than he got caught. He was like a second father. He would always start a conversation, "You know what you should do, Louie?" I know I rolled my eyes at that but he gave good advice. When something wasn't going right in the family, I called Kent. We had lots of laughs. I wish I could have helped him more. I really miss him. Just for the record, Kent eventually turned his life around and he used to lecture at police departments.

I loved playing cribbage with Big Rog, hearing his voice, his jokes, his complaints. He complained just like Dad. "That guy's a sonofabitch. He's a crooked bastard." I miss that about Roger: he was his own man. He didn't care what you thought of him, and I respected that. I wonder if it was smoking that killed him or the fumes from resurfacing the lanes in the bowling alleys. Once I went on the job with him and I could hardly breathe. The only one who could beat Roger in cribbage was his wife, Nettie. He was easily the funniest in the family.

I miss Mary, that smiling face that was so much like mine. We were probably the most alike in the family—both overweight, easy smile, similar temperament, good laugh. She was very funny. She was kind and I'd like to consider myself kind. A big, beautiful, redheaded girl who loved butter as much as you and I did, Mom. When she worked at Porky's drive-in on University Avenue, I wonder if she got razzed a lot because of the name of the place. She married and moved away to Texas and it got more difficult to connect. I could have tried harder, though. I wish I could have got her on a list for a new liver. She was such a good mom. She did the best she could. I say that a lot in life: *She did the best she could, He did the best he could.* But what else can you say? If people could do better, they would, right? Her son, Eugene, sent me some of her jewelry and every time I wear it on *Baskets*, I get to honor her.

And Rhea—God, I loved her. She said that when I showed up, Mom, you would get mad at her because when she came home late, she sometimes went to the room I slept in and pinched me awake so I would play with her. She used to dress me up like a little girl. I'm so glad I went to Connecticut after high school to stay with her for a while. She was so funny, like Roger, and so smart. She would get four or five newspapers every day and read them all. We'd get New York hard rolls and drink coffee. I think I learned about coffee light from her. She knew the history of the family. If she liked you, she'd really go to bat for you. So many of my sisters moved away once they married, and maybe the men wanted them to move, or maybe they did. So many of them chose men like the one you chose, Mom. Rhea was a great mom, too, very protective. She didn't have an easy life. Once, when I was making a family reunion video and I asked Rhea if she could say one thing to Dad, after a pause she said, "I wish I would have been a better daughter." I love Rhea's kids, like I love my other nieces and nephews. One of hers lives in Nevada, so that makes things easier. That's something I'm proud of—I've made an effort at being a good uncle.

Sheila was a stubborn girl. I really loved her. She was skinny, and she suffered, like we all did, from depression, though hers was more severe than some of the others'. Sometimes she left me long voicemails. When she got sick, I felt like she didn't want to be around anymore. She wouldn't quit smoking. I always wanted to scoop her up in my arms and hold her, and I would, and she'd say, "Stop it! Leave me alone!" But she secretly liked it. When her daughter was growing up, Sheila left notes in Tabatha's lunch—"Have a great day," smiley faces, that sort of thing. Sheila would tell her, "Life is good. You'll figure it out." She loved her daughter and adored her grandson and took good care of him. But she had a hard time loving herself, as we all do.

A lot of my older brothers and sisters didn't have easy lives because Dad was even harder on them. When it comes to siblings, as much as you love them, you can do only so much. If they're not going to take care of themselves, you can't force them to. When Sheila would disappear and I'd find her, I'd ask, "Are you smoking?" She'd say, "Yes." At least she didn't bother to lie.

I love them all, Mom. I miss them all. I wish I would have done more, for each and every one of them. Say hello to them for me, if they're with you.

Love,

Louie, Their Kid Brother

Fat Camp

Hey Mom,

I checked into a health "academy"—okay, let's call it what it is, Fat Camp—that had been recommended to me by a friend who had dropped a hundred pounds and looked great. You know, Mom, that I've been through a lot with my weight, and more stuff since you passed. I'm trying to eat healthier, exercise more, see doctors who can help, follow a healthy path. Losing weight would make it easier to get through the TV shoots, because some of those sixteen-hour days are incredibly physically taxing. I'd like to give my legs a little bit of a breather. I considered the sleeve operation, where they cut your stomach in half, but decided against it because I could never get that back again and I wanted another chance to do this on my own. I acknowledged long ago that I'm a food addict, and I realize that I, and those like me, eat for a comfort that can never come from food. It's all about familiarity. Christine Baskets does it, too.

I think Christine has a better body image than Louie Anderson does. Not that hers is great, just better than mine. Not the highest bar in the world.

Anyway, I checked into this health clinic–spa for a couple weeks. I always think I'm dying, so this was as good a time as any. And from what my friend Eddie told me about the place, and the results he got, and what I read, it intrigued me. When I got there I walked around the beautiful grounds. Big lizards running on their hind legs! Had I signed up by accident for Jurassic Park? Were the geckos on the same diet we would all be? It was incredibly hot, so hot my sweat had sweat. August might not have been the best month for this.

There was orientation, then a meet-and-greet circle, where everyone said why they were there. Then they told us not to eat anything because the next morning we would have our blood work done.

I didn't do as much research on the place as I probably should have. Because I soon realized it was a raw vegan place. *Yikes.*

But what the hell! I would give it a try.

The next morning, we had to get our blood taken at 7:00 a.m. I would have preferred having them take it several hours later because I'm not an early-morning person. I think people need more sleep than they think. I know I do. I'm no believer in that "Less sleep is okay" theory.

So at 7:00, they weighed me. I was so fat, more than four hundred pounds, and so tired. Then they took my blood.

I was nervous about what they would find. Which of my several overflow hundred pounds were the problem? When you're that overweight, it means you're sick on some level. Also, it means you eat too much and don't exercise enough.

After the 7:00 a.m. blood work came the 8:00 a.m. breakfast. (There was a schedule for everything.) Lots of vegetables. We got fruit on Mondays, Wednesdays, and Fridays, that's it. Fortunately, it was Friday. I had buckwheat, which tasted sort of like grape nuts only not as good, then some fruit, plus the squirrel stuff you can eat whenever you want. No salt, of course. I think it may be easier to get through life as a raw vegan than as a no-salter. (At least the ocean wasn't far.) There was no sugar, of course. No fat. You couldn't even warm up your food. During my time there, no hot food was allowed except for hot soup. Some people could have hot oatmeal in the morning but almost none of us were part of that privileged class. Actually, it wasn't oatmeal. It was gruel. It was papier-mâché.

They told us that basically everything is bad for you.

Not that I disagree—probably everything *is* bad for you, at least the way America eats—so maybe lots and lots of rules and regulations are exactly what we all need, what I need. The intentions of the people who worked there and ran the place were admirable. They really want their guests to get healthy. They're also suspicious of the medical world and the use of drugs for everyone and chemicals and additives in everything. They believe in focusing on the way we live and what we do, not just what we eat.

After breakfast I spent the next couple hours obsessing about what I was going to have for lunch.

My blood test results were actually not too bad. My cholesterol could be a little better, and my hemoglobin count put me in the pre-diabetes range. But all in all I wasn't terrible. They recommended I drink twenty cups of water a day, as well as three small cups of some green ginger liquid twice a day, and a couple ounces of liquid blue-green algae.

You can't eat meat, of course. Soon enough I was eyeing the geckos skittering around the spa grounds. I mean, for some reason my room came with a toaster oven, yet we couldn't have hot food. So did every single thing have to be eaten raw? If I could catch me one of them lizards and cook it up . . . oh, who was I kidding? On my squirrel diet I was too weak to catch a gecko. But I *did* save 15 percent on my car insurance with Geico.

Mom, why do you think it was so hard for me and all us Andersons to take care of ourselves? Were we missing a certain gene? I don't know what's wrong with us. I don't know why we couldn't do things in moderation, then just, you know . . . stop. Stop overeating. Stop all of our addictions. Addictions really are a disease.

After a week of fat camp I was indoctrinated to believe that all food is poisoning us. All food. Okay, not all food but I'm trying to be dramatic here. Anything that wasn't living, really. If it was cooked, you were cooked. I did learn about some healthy foods that we should eat more of. Do you know how many nutrients are in sprouts? I had no idea. According to the people there, sprouts are at least *forty times more nutritious* than almost anything you can eat. Having a salad? ADD SPROUTS! And there are a hundred different kinds. And then they said that one kind of bean sprout, the mung bean, is the only plant, the only food, ever shown to be effective at halting certain cancers. No . . . Can that be true? I need to do a little research. Why hadn't I heard of it before? Then again, I just learned how to make the text bigger on my iPhone. Now you tell me! After I buy a giant magnifying glass!

They didn't talk just about eating sprouts and all the things you can do with sprouts but also about growing sprouts.

I got so fricking sick of sprouts.

I learned about lots of healthy foods (don't forget about sprouts, though). A lot about taking care of myself. The greatest thing about the spa is that it gave me a chance to really re-think what I was doing with my life and how I was living it. It's true that it's probably much easier to follow strict rules in a very controlled environment because I didn't have to think about the choices I was bombarded with every day, hour, minute, second, the way I do in the real world. Not everyone has the money to try this. In fact, almost no one does. Still, the spa was a very supportive environment, with lots of different things to do. Everyone there was geared to making me feel better, a very positive combination of body, mind, and spirit.

My Mount Rushmore (I used to joke): McDonald's, Pizza Hut, Cold Stone Creamery, Krispy Kreme.

Very early in my stand-up career I did a bit about going to fat camp and competing in the Olympics competition there. "The pole vault? I drove that sucker right into the ground. In gymnastics I did a good thing—straightened out those uneven parallel bars." I did a third joke, which nowadays might be considered a little inappropriate: "The broad jump? I killed her."

Then I capped off the routine with, "After the competition I snuck into the woods to meet a dealer who sold me Snickers."

I was always the fattest boy in class. (I felt so sad for the one girl who was even fatter. When you feel empathy in that situation, that's when you know you're a people pleaser.)

Later, I was the fattest kid everywhere.

I was the fattest person everywhere.

That's no joke.

I added a week to my stay at fat camp, for a total of three weeks. I wasn't ready to return to the real world. The clinic-spa was expensive. I knew I could have done a lot better there than I did. In the first two weeks I'd lost fifteen pounds but probably could have lost forty. It was a good experience but I didn't take proper advantage. I didn't go to all the programs or the meetings—therapy, body manipulation, and more. I didn't exercise as much as I should have. I was lazy some days. I skated through. The spa attracts people from all over, and so many nice ones, and they're all there for the same reasons—to get thinner, to get healthy, to save their life.

In the third and final week I really tried to buckle down, which helped me lose some more weight. I heard about residents who had made great improvements with their triglyceride numbers, who went off their blood pressure medicine, who felt in better balance physically and psychologically. But the big question for me remained: How would I keep it going after I left, and no one was there to run these programs and keep me from being exposed to less healthy food? Does McDonald's simply disappear? Do sprouts automatically get sprinkled on every bite of food? WHERE'S MY BLUE-GREEN ALGAE?? I thought about developing a sitcom about a place like the fat camp spa, with characters from the worlds of both the staff and guests. I liked the coming together and clashing of these two groups—normal "real life" and this fantasy world of perfect health and energy that we all *say* we want but we hate doing the work to get there.

Still, even just a few weeks at such a place changes the way you think about almost everything, not only about eating but how you treat yourself as a person, how people look at you, how you let them look at you, whether you accept that or push back against it, what parts of your childhood and upbringing you carry with you, often damaging baggage, wherever you go and whatever you do, a great reminder that we are, ultimately, in control of so much about our lives. And just because we forget it or ignore it or overlook it or put it at the bottom of our to-do list, never to rise to the top, doesn't make it any less so.

On "graduation day," one of the guests, a French woman, stood and said simply, in heavily accented English, "This place is so special," then stopped talking and began singing, without accompaniment, "La Vie en Rose."

I don't have to tell you how many dry eyes were in the house, Mom.

Love,

Your son, the Hungry Hungry Hippo Louie

My World

Hey Mom,

I work a lot. Did you know that about me? Did I seem that driven when I was younger? I don't know if you would call me a workaholic but I have a very heavy touring schedule. Over the last two years, I did close to two hundred shows of stand-up. For the last two years I've been one of the main actors on *Baskets*. I just became a regular guest panelist on the syndicated TV game show *Funny You Should Ask*. I'm shooting a new comedy special in November. I guess you could call me ambitious, though I really want to figure out a way to do all my work while lying down. (The game show I'm on almost accomplishes that: I call it *Hollywood Squares in Chairs* because my fellow comedian-panelists and I just sit in our chairs and deliver funny lines cooked up for us by talented, funny writers. And they pay me to do this?)

I have at least five books I want to write after *Hey Mom*, if this actually becomes a book. (Trust me, Mom, when I say that this one here would be the most important to me.) And I don't plan on rushing the others because I know it's important to let good ideas sit. I already wrote three books, including *Dear Dad*. I guess I'm not the only one trying to make sense of growing up with a volatile alcoholic parent because not only was the book a bestseller but, as I wrote you earlier, I got so many letters from readers.

Maybe my desire to create comes from Grandpa Alfred Anderson, Dad's dad, the inventor, who had more than fifty patents to his name, including for the clamp clothespin, a railway switch, a version of a stove hood, a mechanism for opening and closing doors, and a deep fryer. Hopefully, I don't take after him completely, since he squandered his money so badly on drunken trips with Grandma Engaborg and they neglected their family until it was ruined.

Can I tell you about my biggest idea, Mom, much bigger than the others?

I call it MyWorld.

It's a website to change the world. I know, I sound full of myself. But I really think it can save the world. So you would think I would be working harder on it, right? (Remember, I may be ambitious but I also just want to lie down.) Anyway, the idea first came to me in a dream. I think the reason it came to me like that was because once, *not* in a dream, I overheard someone say, "Websites are living, breathing animals, they feel like they're alive when you go to them," and that idea hit me deeply, and it probably squirmed into my subconscious.

Okay, the idea. You wake up in the morning and before you do anything (fine, you can have some coffee or juice, maybe a cinnamon roll or a banana) you log on to a site called MyWorld (or whatever name close to that is available). A world comes up—an image of the Earth. A globe that has your name at the top. You can rotate it. As you turn it, you see "problem flags," things you would like to see changed, remedied, improved, eliminated—really big problems and issues like climate change, human trafficking, access to clean water, hunger, genocide, destruction of rain forests, mental health care, care for wounded soldiers, etc., etc. You see images or videos showing the problem, and situated right where it's most a problem—so you can see a faucet dripping with just a few drops of water in sub-Saharan Africa, and you see the rain forest being cut away in the Amazon. You also see all the wonderful things in the world that you want to see more of or be part of or create: exotic travel, gorgeous settings, beautification projects, etc. Now, to make sure that you don't get overwhelmed trying to save the whole world and fix *every* problem, you see only those issues that you selected to be involved with. And whenever you log in, other people can see your profile, and know which problems you care most about, just like you can see everyone else's. Yes, it's a little like Facebook. (Remember Facebook, Mom?) And you and the people who care about the same problems and issues can join in helping to solve them—thousands of people, hopefully millions—which makes you feel like you're shrinking the world just a little bit. Because, let's face it, this is a big project. It's hard to fix or improve even one of these problems, and part of the reason is because it all feels way too big, so why bother? Maybe by looking at your world in this way it would change how you woke up in the morning, and how millions of others felt when they woke up. I also want to get charities and corporations involved, as well as the one thousand most influential people in the world, some of whom, I realize, because of their wealth and power and agendas, are not exactly what we would call "the good guys." But we have to get as many people involved as possible if we're going to make a real dent in these problems. It's about inclusion. It's about looking at things in a more manageable way.

I have to go lie down now.

Does everyone dream about saving the world? Being a catcher in the rye? I have another idea, for an animated series called *Louie*

Saves the World, where Louie, a comedian, goes to the big city to do stand-up—but it's really just a ruse because his mission is to save someone, do something.

MyWorld. Think how good you would feel if you woke up and dealt with even one of the issues plaguing the world every day, especially when it's an issue that matters to you. We all have something that matters to us.

MyWorld is my new way to look at the world. It's a canvas we're all trying to paint, together. It's a living, breathing animal but we're not just content to keep it living and breathing. We want it flourishing.

I have other ideas, Mom, but that's enough for now. I'm going to finish this letter, then have a healthy snack. *Then* save the world.

Entrepreneurially yours,

Louie

Family Peace

Hey Mom,

The *Family Feud* producers called to ask me to participate in an episode of the show with our family as contestants! With Steve Harvey hosting! Of course I said we would do it!

Me, Jimmy, his son James, Nettie, and Valerie.

And we were absolutely terrible.

We got crushed by the other team. I was particularly bad. I was under the weather the night we taped, and I thought I let everyone down.

But after the show, Nettie came up to me.

"Louie, this is a dream come true," she said. "I will never forget it. I've always wanted to do this."

"Why didn't you tell me?" I asked. After all, I'd been the host for three years.

"Oh, I didn't want to say anything," she said. What a sweet woman. No wonder Roger loved her so much.

And that moment with Nettie, Mom, made me very happy and also a little sad. Her dream had come true and I had helped to make that happen—but it also made me realize how often people don't express their dreams, whatever they may be, however small or big. We should probably say what our dreams are every day, speak them out loud, in the presence of others, or they can get buried or forgotten. Why would people need to probe you with questions to find out what you're dreaming? That shouldn't be. We should be transparent about our dreams, to others and ourselves. Never assume that people, even those you're close to and who love you and who you love, will just volunteer their most important aspirations and thoughts.

Is that why I'm asking you so many questions, Mom? Because I fear you lived your life without fulfilling some of your dreams? Most of your dreams?

Love,

Louie

Hat Day

© FX

Hey Mom,

Last year I started this thing on Instagram called "Hat Day Sunday." (Instagram, Mom: Remember the slideshows we had to watch of relatives' vacations? Same thing, except now you watch it in private and don't have to fake emotions about the pictures. And it's not just pictures of vacations but things like salads and rustic doorknobs.) I just love doing Hat Day Sunday and lots of people out there seem to like it, too. Every Sunday now I post a picture of either me or someone I know wearing a hat. Everybody should have a day where they wear a hat. Hats are wonderful things. Hats don't get enough credit. They transform you from one person to another, one profession to another. You get to be someone else. Hats give you cover if it's raining or snowing. If it's windy they hide a case of bad hair day or bedhead. Mom, did we use the expression "bedhead"? Hats are underrated. When you wear your favorite sports team's cap, sometimes you're saying a lot but sometimes not. Because hats don't have to mean anything, either. They're just fun. Look at my Instagram, @louieanderson, and you can see all the Sunday hats. Or even better, put on your best or most favorite hat and send me the picture.

Who am I talking to, Mom? You don't have an Instagram account.

Besides great hat pictures, I continue to get great responses from your—I mean, Christine's—admirers, who share with me stories about their moms:

> *Baskets* and your character Christine came into my life at a time when I desperately needed laughter. I was pregnant and had also just been diagnosed with breast cancer. It was a scary time and the doctors kept stressing to me that I needed to really try hard to keep my anxiety down for mine and the baby's sake. So I watched a lot of *Baskets* lol. I've probably watched each episode a dozen times. I'm happy to say I'm cancer-free now with a healthy 16-month-old little boy. But I wanted to thank you for getting me through a very tough time in my life!
>
> My mom story:
>
> She very much reminded me of Christine! I lost her to breast cancer when she was 47 and I was 21. She was a very conservative Christian lady and didn't listen to much music outside of Christian artists. But she LOVED the song "Gangsta's Paradise"

by Coolio! I can still picture her dancing and rapping along with the song. Such a random thing but it's still one of my favorite memories of her.

Rebecca Bennett

My favorite memory of my mother took place in the 1970s.

We lived in a rural town. We had fruit trees, grape vines, an enormous vegetable garden, and horses. It sounds idyllic, but it wasn't really.

I had very good parents, but my father was very controlling. He had been an abused child and it manifested itself in him wanting to have mastery over his environment. He picked out my mother's outfits each day, took her income and gave her no allowance or access to the checkbook, and kept her from getting a driver's license. He had the neighborhood kids so spooked, they all would get quiet near our house so they would not upset him.

My father provided well. My mother, thanks to him, looked like Jacqueline Onassis, but if she needed eggs or milk, she had to ask for them.

My flamboyant and demonstrative uncle sent me two kites, among other goodies, for my birthday one year, but no kite string. So the kites were mounted on my bedroom wall for a long time. We lived in a rural area and really could not walk to a store, and we did not dare ask my father for kite string.

So my mother, and I am tearing up as I type this, tied every piece of yarn and string we had in the house and made perhaps a twenty foot kite string perfect for a small paper kite. And we went outside, and by God, we tried to fly that little yellow kite.

My father died in 2001. I forgave him. He could not help himself. I can say I love him.

My mother lives with me now. She is my friend and I love her.

Regards,
Johnny Michnay

Fellow Minnesotan here, with my mom story, one of many: I was about four years old and my mother had three daughters four and under. I was born in 1960, my sister in 1961 and my little sister 1963. I remember clearly not being happy when my little sister showed up. It was like my mom had no time for me and I hated this little screaming thing that was taking all of my mom's attention. So I acted out a lot. I was a brat! I would make scenes in the grocery store. You name it. I'm sure I made a stressful time in her life even more stressful.

We lived in Elgin, Illinois. It was a beautiful summer day when my mom took me for a car ride. I think she dropped my sisters at my grandmother's but I don't remember that part. We drove to a huge red brick building with lots of children in uniforms playing in the front yard. She pulled me out of the car and said, This is where children that do not have parents go.

She quickly got into the car and drove off. She had driven around the block, which I didn't know at the time. I remember the clear sunny day. I remember the children. I remember the building. I remember the tree-lined street. I remember crying so hard tears and snot ran into my mouth. I remember feeling so horrible for how I had been treating my mother.

She may have left me there a minute or two but it seemed like a lifetime. She drove up and I hopped into the car. I don't remember the drive home but I remember the relief in seeing her pull up to pick me up.

My dad to this day can't talk about it without getting red in the face. But it was one of the best things that has ever happened to me. I had no idea there were children without parents. It's not that I became the perfect kid, I still got in trouble, but it changed me and made me even at 4 appreciate all that I have. I tell her often how thankful I am that she did that.

I found an old postcard on eBay of the orphanage, which I keep on my refrigerator.

Thank you, momma.

A big fan,
Becky Meverden

Doing What We Shouldn't,
Not Doing What We Should

Hey Mom,

Why are people so careless with something so precious, for a potential return of something so silly?

It takes a split second to smash into the back of a car while texting. Talking on the phone isn't much better except the talker usually doesn't look at a screen. A split second—for what? You can't take it back. Yeah, maybe the texter-driver texted perfectly 99,999 times, with no typos or mangled bodies or mischosen emojis or future charges of vehicular homicide. But the next time, the very next time, there could be death. That's all it takes. Just once. I tell my Lyft drivers, "If you look at your phone one more time, I'm asking for another driver!" And when they put it down it doesn't make me happy. No, it makes me angry. Because they just proved that they *can* put it down. They just don't. Ever. This habit, this addiction, this itch we all think we have to scratch—it's none of that. They can put it down while they're driving. They can put it down most of the time. We all can. Stop it, we can. Stop kidding around, we can.

But we don't.

Why do we believe that the laws of physics and the impact of a metal box moving at seventy miles an hour on flesh and bone will somehow halt, like a game of freeze tag, because we want to respond to a non-urgent message with another non-urgent message?

Then there's the other problem: thinking that time stops. (Switching lanes, I know.)

I'll get to it. I'll do it. It won't be that long. I just have to put some time aside. I'm going to write that book. I'm going to visit that person, I'm going to figure that out . . .

We all say all these things. Then we wake up one day and say, "Wait, *what* was I going to do?"

I'm just rambling, Mom. What other subjects should I go on about? The college football playoff system? Olives with pits? There's a lot out there that's just painful to witness, so I'm cranky, wanting things to be better, people to be better, like you wanted, but I'm not sure they will get better, or can get better. No, that's not right, they can . . . but will they? Will I? Can I take each day, Mom, and stay on the straight and narrow? Stay on the path that's healthy? Where I'm not acting hangry? Isn't "hangry" a great word, Mom? Hungry + Angry = Hangry. I love some of the new words we have today, Mom, like *spam* (remember we used to eat Spam? Not the kind that clogs up my computer, the kind you used to fry up in a pan)*, meh, selfie, snail mail*, and *staycation*. I prefer a *laycation* myself. That's where you go from one place where you were lying down to another place to lie down, and so on.

Was I complaining before? Should I stop it? Wasn't that one of the promises I made to myself?

No matter what we try to do, if we're not careful we always end up back in the trough. Back at the Dairy Queen, back at the Soft Serve, back at the Slurpee, back at the nacho bar.

Is this about me or everyone?

Big questions, Mom. I should just stick to the basics. Keep it simple.

Parents should love their children.

Children should enjoy being young.

When you hit forty, you should climb something, anything, because soon you might not be able to.

The things that taste best are always the worst for your health and should be eaten in moderation except in times of extreme anxiety.

And women should be in charge of everything. Honestly, Mom, I feel that way. If women were completely in charge, or way more in charge than they currently are, first hunger and then homelessness and human trafficking would be eliminated. I bet drug-related crimes would go down, too. I just feel that. Clean water for one and all. Everyone would have clean clothes, clean underwear. Three squares a day. Every toilet seat would be put back down. Everybody would have to go to bed by nine o'clock.

Looking at myself, too,

Louie

Big Underwear

Hey Mom,

One day I was pulling clothes out of my dryer and folding my underwear and I said out loud, "Damn! These are gigantic!"

And a comedy bit was born.

They were absolutely gigantic. And even though I was alone in my own house, I imagined all of this happening in a community laundromat, and me yelling, "Are these mine?"

At some point later, I was going through a storage space and came across five or six boxes of underwear. A small city of underwear, because I remember when I was growing up I had just one or two pairs, and I so appreciate that you did the laundry every day, Mom, maybe every couple days at most, so that we would always have clean underwear. And here I have these boxes and boxes of underwear, unused, forgotten. I actually tried to give the underwear away, only I found out you can't. Goodwill said they wouldn't take it.

"It's unsanitary," the Goodwill guy told me on the phone.

"It's not dirty underwear," I said. "It's not *used* underwear. It's new."

"Sorry," he said.

Too bad, I thought. *Think of all the Louie-sized homeless people that could be using this underwear.*

I decided to make artwork out of it.

I decided to make a routine out of it.

I decided I would do a bit about it at the Comedy Store when I was in L.A.

I decided to title my next TV special *Big Underwear*.

Thanks for always keeping me and Tommy and the rest of us in clean underwear, Mom, when we were too poor to have boxes and boxes of it.

You're a great mom, Mom,

Louie

When It Rains, It Pours

Hey Mom,

Loss is always just around the corner. It's part of every life, lying in wait for us. I've had this theory for most of my adult life (I wrote about it in *Dear Dad*): that *all* we deal with in life is loss. We just keep losing—the comfort of the womb, access to our mother's breast, the "luxury" to mess in our pants; we lose family members, friends, teachers, neighbors, our hair, our teeth, our speed, our flexibility, our youth. We lose them, don't get them back, and don't know how to deal with these losses because we haven't been taught how. We won't admit (most of us, anyway) how much it hurts. In many ways, often more subconscious than conscious, we spend all our lives trying to alleviate the feeling of loss, often grasping tightly to things we should let go of. We should always hug each other tighter because of the presence of loss, because loss is there to remind us to live every minute fully and enjoy it like it's the last dark chocolate buttercream caramel or dark chocolate truffle or milk chocolate pecan/English walnut cluster in the box of Russell Stover candy, *to name a few*.

Because I had to say something upbeat when talking about loss.

The world is full of sorrow right now, but maybe always. Probably. No, definitely always. I live with sorrow every day because I see it everywhere. Last night I had a job performing for a company that transports individuals and families from one side of the globe to the other. They take you and all your stuff, all the way down to your toothbrush, from St. Paul, Minnesota, to Dubai, or from Paris, Texas, to Paris, France, or vice versa, or from Boston to Austin or Nebraska to Alaska or Malta to Yalta. (Sorry.) Afterward, I had a meet and greet, and took hundreds of photos with people. What autographs were a generation ago, Mom, that's what these celebrity photos are now. (Did I just call myself a celebrity? Ugh.) Did you ever get any autographs, Mom? Did you get one from Dad that first night you saw him play trumpet with Hoagy Carmichael's band and fell in love with him? I know you and your mom and your dad listened to the radio as Lindbergh crossed the Atlantic, and we all watched the moon landing on TV together. So anyway, after the show for the moving company, I was riding high, carrying my leftovers and walking to the car they sent for me. I remember how much you enjoyed it when they sent a car for us when I was filling in for Joan Rivers because her husband, Edgar, had committed suicide. Joan was feeling sorrow then and maybe forever after because suicide is a brutal thing. You just don't know what to do! Who to be mad at. When someone commits suicide, here's the question I always have: Who did they want to kill? I know Dad's sister killed herself because of the murder at their house years earlier, which ultimately caused Dad such agony, and his agony caused you and all your children such agony. Do you think it was smart for me not to have kids, Mom? Sorrow is like plastic in the environment: it takes years for it to dissipate. SpellCheck wants to say *disappear* or *dissolve* instead of *dissipate* but I'm not gonna let it, Mom, *I'm not gonna let SpellCheck win!* Sorrow is like a sparrow: Out of nowhere it can land right in front of you. Though luckily it can also be gone in an instant.

On this beautiful Chicago evening I was feeling no sorrow, I had a great show, people laughing and cheering me on, uplifting comments during the photo taking, from "I'm a longtime fan!" to "I loved *Life with Louie*!" to "I love your stuff about your parents! I love your mom character on *Baskets*!!"

At the Waldorf Astoria Chicago, I went up to my room, had some dinner, and decided I needed a shower, to relax. In hotels I always ask for a handicap bathroom because the showers are better to walk into—bigger, less slippery, and the older you get, the more you need a railing. Plus, there's a chair that folds out from the wall that you can sit on. I turned the water on and just let it run over me. I was really enjoying my shower. There's something about a really nice hot shower that brings you anywhere you want to go. It gives you a chance to wipe away some of what's racing in your mind after a show, an entertainer's quick path to meditation. I got the show, I got the laughs, I got the check, I got to meet a lot of wonderful people. I knew I was a lucky guy.

Then a creak and a crash.

Before I knew it I had pulled the chair out of the wall and was lying on the shower floor. I rolled over, half laughing and half crying. The water continued to run over me. I was very afraid I might not be able to get up. Here I was, an entry on Comedy Central's list of 100 Greatest Stand-Ups of All Time, 420 pounds, and I couldn't even stand up. I was lying on the shower floor, the entire seat pulled out of the shower wall.

My first instinct was to blame someone—but who? There must have been a warning on the chair but I couldn't see one. What was the top weight the chair was good for—300 pounds? 350? 400? 450? As the numbers climbed in my head, I realized, in that moment, what I had thought I'd realized so many, many times before: I have to do something about this. I felt a range of emotions—embarrassment, shame, fear, rage, self-loathing . . . but really sorrow.

How did this happen? How do you get like this? This was definitely my next journey, I thought, while lying there, water pounding my body. This time I'll complete it. Sometimes you just know you're going to do a good job cutting the lawn, washing the car, cleaning the fridge, writing a book report . . . you just know.

It was time. I felt it. Humiliation and desperation are powerful motivators. A lot of people are going to say to me, "You look really good—but aren't you worried you won't be funny?"

When I hear that, my answer will be very simple. "No, I'm not worried at all," I'll say.

I got up off the floor—I don't even remember how, though I believe I reached for a towel and grabbed the handles of the shower and somehow got my footing. As much as anything, I willed myself up. And when I stood, I took a good long look at myself in the mirror. I said goodbye to that body. I said hello to my new life. I walked into the bedroom, picked up the bag of M&M's that I'd taken from the mini-bar and tossed on the bed, waiting to be devoured, and returned them to the mini-bar. No more M&M's for me. I told myself I was going to try to live on really healthy food and lots of laughs, love, gratitude, and humility.

I'm going to do whatever I have to do, Mom.

Love,

Soaking Wet Louie

12-Step

Hey Mom,

I'm back in a 12-step program. I rejoined last week, on April 15, after a friend said to me, "Hey, Louie, are you gonna just fricking kill yourself? Because if you're gonna just fricking kill yourself, I don't really want to be around to watch. If you don't give a damn about you, *I'm* not going to give a damn about you."

I woke up. I mean, it's not the first wake-up call I've had in my life, and I think we all have a lot more wake-up calls than we recognize or are willing to acknowledge. But my friend's words were pretty harsh and totally on the money. You hate it when people say things to you like what he said to me, especially if it's a person who cares about you, but it stuck. I have to look at where I am. I want to be around for a while. I want to be the best Louie I can be.

I'm exercising more. I do stuff for my chest, back, both arms, both legs, both stomachs. Three to four times a week, three to four sets for each body part. For a while I've had a lifetime membership to Anytime Fitness because I did some commercials for them, and when I'm there sometimes I work with a trainer. When I'm on the road I have this WeGym equipment, this little thing that you pull. I lay it out on the counter of my hotel room and pretend I'm going to use it. Sometimes I keep the door open with it. Sometimes I actually use it.

This time I hope I keep my commitment to the program. I really, really want to. I'm not gonna lie: it's going to get bumpy, like now, when I'm in a hotel, and there's a stocked mini-bar and I want to eat all the food in front of me—let's see, there's a giant bag of potato chips, gummy bears, peanuts, those damn M&M's, cashews, three different types of cookies, and that's just what I can see from across the room. That's just the stuff that's speaking to me! I really am only noticing it now. They would be easy pickings, these goodies, and not one of them can do me any good. Not one of them can help me. Maybe the cashews but they're probably processed in some way. So I have to make that choice. If I wasn't on the program and in the right space, my mind would bring me back to these all night long. Yeah, I could rationalize having the "healthiest" item, the cashews, but it's not on my program.

"Is this room service? Can I get some carrots and some celery? And a side of disappointment?"

Mom, I hope this is some kind of turning point. And I need to share it with you.

I mostly wanted you to know that I'm eating healthier, trying to avoid fast food and processed food, and trying to manage what I consume. I build in snacks and make them healthy snacks, like an apple. I'm in a better state of mind, though I know it's a day-to-day thing. I honestly don't feel threatened by the hotel candies and cookies.

Though I might just ask them to remove it all tomorrow, for safety's sake.

Love,

Louie

Fellowship

Dad

Hey Mom,

    I'm on my way home from a meeting of my fellowship group, where all of us have one problem in common: food. For me and you, Mom, it was food. For Dad, it was drinking. I like bread way more than I like booze—yet both are made from grains. And both can kill. Are grains killing us all? Are they the most acceptable drug of choice for us Americans? It's the grain drain!

I remember when Dad went to an AA meeting, and the hopeful feeling as I considered, *Is it really possible that soon I could have a nicer, more understanding, loving father?* Some of us also went to an Al-Anon meeting (not Dad, though), for the loved ones of alcoholics, because when someone is an alcoholic everyone around is affected—I mean *infected*. I loved that Al-Anon meeting in particular, and I think you liked it, Mom. It made me feel as if I wasn't the only one with a drunk for a father.

Dad went to a grand total of . . . one AA meeting.

"I don't need any fricking help to quit drinking," he said. I don't know that he used the word *fricking*.

To his credit, though he never went to another meeting, he quit drinking. He never drank again after that. Problem was, he totally white-knuckled it. To Dad's *dis*credit, his behavior didn't change much. Yeah, he wasn't as mean, especially to you, Mom, but he discovered new kinds of mean, new kinds of cruel. He was arbitrary about tasks we kids had to perform. There was no way he would be satisfied with the result, no matter how good and painstaking. If you cut the grass up and back, he'd say he'd wanted it cut in circles. Make him a sandwich, and guaranteed you had put the meat and cheese in the wrong order. One day he liked mustard, the next day he didn't. And all of the demands accompanied by a "What are you, a fricking moron?" I don't know that he used the word *fricking*.

We never went to another Al-Anon meeting, even though I liked that first one.

That was more than forty-five years ago, those initial meetings. I'm glad I'm going to these fellowship meetings now. I go at least once a week. It makes me feel less alone. I'm living a healthier life.

I'm healing a giant part of me. I'm just sorry it took so many years to really take care of myself.

But better late than never, right, Mom?

What failed with Dad maybe won't fail with me.

Your healthier & happier son,

Louie

It's Your Faults, Mom

Hey Mom,

You're the loveliest person I ever knew and I was so fortunate that it was you I had for a mother. But it wouldn't be right if I didn't point out at least a couple of your faults. Okay with you, Mom?

You enabled a lot of Dad's behavior. Yes, I understand what a difficult situation you were put in, with eleven kids and being poor and the times being what they were. But you were an enabler. When Dad quit drinking at sixty-nine, you said, "I told you he'd quit."

I was speechless when I heard that. I didn't say anything to you at the time. I was seventeen years old and I remember I just walked into my room and sat on the bed and said to myself, or maybe I even mumbled it out loud, "Oh my God, she thinks that she got him to quit, at sixty-nine."

You sometimes said to me and the other kids, "It'll get better," about Dad and our situation, and you knew it was a lie. But you told yourself it was true. You told us it was. And we could see through it.

I understand that Dad lived in denial much of the time—like when he got diagnosed with prostate cancer and refused to get it treated—and simply never confronted his innermost fears, at least in a constructive way that could have benefited his family (and him). I have tried to go a very different route but I'm not sure you weren't more like him than me.

We were poorer than you wanted to admit, Mom.

And sometimes it seemed as if you wanted to talk only about the kids who were doing well.

You had a vain streak. Not that it bothered me very much, and I've incorporated it into Christine's character, and I think vanity is sometimes overcriticized, because it's really a cry for dignity and respect, maybe because self-respect is lacking. But you did have your vain moments. Don't we all? "Louie, how old do you think I look?" I always guessed under because I knew, Mom, that that's what you were fishing for. I started doing it myself, asking people to guess how old I looked, but quit when somebody got it right.

Mirror, mirror, on the wall, who's the vainest of them all? Maybe both of us, Mom. (Yeah, everyone is at least a little vain. If they're not, I don't trust them.)

More than once, Mom, you actually said, "Be a good child, Louie. Don't cause problems. Don't act up. We don't want your father to start drinking."

If you'll pardon my French, Mom: what bullshit.

One part of you that I've thoroughly incorporated into Christine: passive-aggressiveness. No one does it with more genius than a Middle American, middle-aged woman. That way of sliding something in that's really pure competitiveness and often vindictiveness and a kind of showing off, but is supposed to look nothing like it. Is anything more passive-aggressive and Middle American than the expression, "Well, isn't that something?"

In my act, I used to say that Midwesterners will cut you with a razor, then say, "Oh my word, let me go get you my first aid kit, I don't know what got into me!" My theory? It's so cold, we stay in the house too long.

And then you lived by a code that has always left me puzzled, maybe enough to make me want to write a whole book to figure it out, while also celebrating how much I love you. That code?

Everyone should tell the truth as long as it doesn't hurt people's feelings.

Is that even possible, Mom?

I used to blame you, Mom. *Why did you put me—us—through this horrible time with our father? Why wouldn't you protect us? Why wouldn't you call the National Guard, the militia, the police?* I used to blame you. *Why didn't you do that, Mom? What were you thinking? What kind of a mother would do that to her children?*

But that was a younger Louie, a less empathetic Louie. A less life-experienced Louie. A Louie who had experienced less loss, less disappointment, less success. Once I started looking at myself, I understood. It came into greater focus just how hard it must have been for you. I bet you agonized over it all, internalized it enough to cause eleven ulcers in your one stomach. I wonder if the sleeve operation helps you get rid of ulcers?

You took the blows for us. You stood in front of the firing squad every day for us.

I hope you won't be angry with me for pointing out these flaws. We all have them, most of us way more than you. It only makes you more human and lovable, really.

With apologies,

Louie

Writers Need Deadlines

Hey Reader,

I started out writing these simple letters to my mom but then I sent them to a few friends and they seemed to enjoy them and said I should write a book of them, which you'll remember I was sort of thinking about but not with great seriousness. So I said okay, because "okay" didn't mean I had to do it; "okay" is about as non-committal as you can get. ("We'll see" is the king of non-committal. But "okay" is close.) Then I sent a few of the letters to a few publishers and each of them I met with wanted the book. Which was a good feeling and a bad feeling, because it meant they liked it and it also meant I had to finish it. If you commit to writing sixty-five thousand words, then you've got to write all sixty-five. Thousand. Words. Down. *And*—get this—*they've got to be in the right order! And make sense!* So I went from being anxious if anyone would even want to read these letters to anxious about producing them and finishing them. And even more anxious as the days went by because I now have to have this book done by November 1 and it's already October. I have my phone on mute a lot these days. Anyway, if I didn't have a deadline, I probably wouldn't finish it, so fortunately (ha!) I have one. I think deadlines were started by moms and dads. There are soft deadlines, maybe more from moms: "Clean your room, honey, because I don't want to keep walking by here and seeing this mess." And then not-so-soft ones, maybe more from dads: "You're not leaving this house until you finish mowing the lawn!" ("How am I going to mow the lawn if I can't leave the house?") There are office deadlines: "I'd like to have that report by Friday, Louie!" ("I'm sure you would, and I'd like to have an ice cream sundae but there's no ice cream and it's not Sunday!" "That's good, Louie, just get the report to me by Friday.") And there are show business deadlines: "We have to finish shooting this scene by four thirty, drop-dead latest." "Why?" "That's when the sun starts setting." "But the scene takes place in a basement." "It's just a basement. There's no house there."

We need deadlines. I'm glad I have a deadline to finish this book.

I have a question for you—you, reader, not my mom, but you: When are you going to contact, surprise, hug the people you love?

That's my deadline for everyone. Just like I should have been a lot nicer and more loving to my mom and should have done more for her, and then she was gone, here's my deadline for whoever's out there:

Call your mom. Call your dad.

Call your sister. Call your brother.

Call your son. Call your daughter.

Make plans for dinner with them.

Go have lunch with them. It can be breakfast, if that's your preference.

Give them some of the time they've given you. Sometimes even give them time they *haven't* given you.

Don't be one of those people who starts weeping with regret every time they hear Harry Chapin's "Cat's in the Cradle" or *Fiddler on the Roof*'s "Sunrise, Sunset." I mean, if you're over forty years old you'll weep anyway but don't be one of those people who weeps so hard that everyone within fifty yards starts getting uncomfortable.

You won't regret taking the time now rather than later. It's impossible to regret that. But if you don't do it now, when you can, you will regret it later, when you can't.

Trust me on that.

One more thing I know for sure: Only a very small group of people are truly taking in what I just wrote. I hope you're in that group. I was once one of those not in that group, and I didn't listen until I was absolutely forced to, and in some ways it was too late.

Can't discuss this with you anymore—gotta get back to work. Sixty-five thousand words is a lot of words. But thanks for letting me spill about seven hundred more of them right here.

Love you, whoever you are,

Serious Louis, on deadline

This Book Is Not About You, Dad, Except When It Is

Hey Mom,

Today, I got to see the ten scripts for Season 3 of *Baskets* and there's a scene, in Episode 3, taken exactly from our life. Last year I told this story to Jonathan, the director, and the Season 3 writers, and they decided it was perfect to incorporate. Instead of happening to me, which it did, now it happens to young Christine Baskets, in a flashback. So, remember the time when Dad got so drunk (I know, which time, right?), then insisted on driving back home through the snow, with Tommy and me in the car? And I pleaded with him not to but he wouldn't listen? And then, as he was nodding off, he accidentally floored the gas and the car shot through the wooded area in front of our house—where we used to pick raspberries in summer and slide down the snow in winter—and now branches were getting hacked off as our car plowed through the snowy woods until we crashed into a tree? And Dad just snored through it all, and I had to go get help from home before Dad and Tommy froze? I got out of the car and scampered up the hill but it was icy and I slid down, and I tried again and I slid down, and the third time I went up I knew I was going to slide down and I just went "Whee!" and almost forgot that Dad had just driven us into a tree and almost killed Tommy and me?

Yeah, that time.

Anyway, there's a scene like that in the show now where young Christine is pleading with her alcoholic father to not drive, but he does, because that's what drunks do, and she's in the car with him, and they plow into a hospital. And she has to take charge and go get help.

Fact and fiction.

My own explanations of my childhood—what's fact and what's fiction?

Dad was a veteran. That's a fact. Doesn't matter whose point of view. It's fact. World War I. Bugler.

But how much that fact affected his behavior, and how much he still controlled—that's no fact anymore. Or maybe there's more than one set of facts. No, forget that, Mom. I don't want to put it that way. Sounds too much like "fake news." (Mom, I won't even bother explaining that to you this time around.)

Dad was funny but I don't think I can call that a fact because it was almost always mean-funny, which is not everyone's cup of tea. "Louie, you've got a point. Too bad it's at the top of your head." Or "I think you're a really great person . . . so far." Funny, yes, but mean-funny.

And when he maintained sobriety for the last decade of his life—it's a *fact* that he didn't take another drink. (Okay, that's technically not true: there was that one time in the casino when he was so sick with cancer and he was playing the dime slot machine and they came around offering free drinks and he ordered a cold beer and I kept my mouth shut, though I was upset.) But is it a *fact* that we were better off this way? From whose perspective? In many ways, he was just as cruel, only in a different way. He was innovating new ways to be an a-hole!

As kids, Dad and his sister were taken away from their parents after a murder occurred in their home during a party, with the parents nowhere to be found. Dad and Olga were put up in front of the local church. (That's the root of the phrase, "put up for adoption.") They were chosen by separate families and split up forever. Dad's new "family" basically wanted an unpaid farmhand. They made him live in the attic. In some important ways, he was a better person than either of his reckless parents, biological and adoptive.

But what do I do with these facts or fictions? Do I forgive him? Yes, I forgive him. Do I think I understand him? In some ways, yes, in some ways, never. Is it better, Mom, that you didn't leave him, didn't divorce him, didn't get on with your life and our eleven lives? Only you can answer that. For years and years I've told myself that I understand why you didn't, it was the times, and we were poor, and there were just so many mouths to feed and—and this is not a small thing—you still loved him. In a way, you always adored him. But I didn't get the nurturing, quality encouragement that a kid needs from a dad, that a son needs from his dad. I did get to be in his sunlight, though, and even sunlight that doesn't always shine bright is better than no sunlight at all. Would I be as funny as I am and as successful as I am, and be doing this thing that I absolutely love doing, if I hadn't been exposed to him and the relentlessness of his cruelty to us? I doubt it. If he hadn't treated me like that, would I have searched so long and hard to find something to explain it all or something to make me feel better? Maybe that's what makes the comedy. Your stick of butter, Mom, plus his gallon of vinegar. Should I cut him slack simply because he was also the kind of guy who would get into a big fight with someone, then go buy groceries and leave them on the doorstep of someone else who was struggling worse than we were?

I don't know, Mom. He was the good, the bad, and the ugly, rolled into one.

Maybe that's who all of us are, only in different measures.

I know I can't get him out of my head, either, and writing a book about him didn't change things completely, like I could put that all to rest. Just this week I met with producers from the Strand Theater in San Francisco, and they offered me the chance to "workshop" *Dear Dad* and help me to take it from the page to the stage. Crazily, I said yes. And I have this idea where at each performance we ask a few theatergoers to be part of the show by each reading one of the letters I wrote to him in that book. And in the lobby would be a display of the letters and all these photographs from Dad's life and when he was a younger man and a trumpet player in Hoagy Carmichael's band and things seemed a little brighter for him, or maybe not, given what his own childhood was like, and there would be a trumpet player playing me on and off stage and during crucial scenes, too. A trumpet blaring while I'm reading about being tortured by my father.

If things go well, maybe that journey will end up taking me and Dad, and you and the rest of our family, to Broadway.

I know this, Mom: when that book came out, I did a bunch of interviews promoting it, and one interviewer asked me, "Louie, would you trade all that happened then and since for a normal childhood?"

And to that question, then and now, I always say . . .

Yes.

Simple: I've already had the unhappy childhood. Why not give the happy one a go?

Sorry—though I don't think I need to apologize,

Louie

Reunion

Family gathering in Woodbury, Minnesota

Hey Mom,

I just returned from our Anderson Family Reunion! What a beautiful day!

Jimmy and Janice set it up. We had it at Keller Park and because it rained most of the day, it was a good thing we were under one of the pavilions. It was a great setup. Jimmy had it catered, then everybody put in some money to help. Jimmy, my last remaining brother, has the perfect makeup for helping to pull this all together—a loving soul with a great work ethic. And—again—he's your favorite, Mom.

We had quite the turnout!

It always makes me happy to see everyone. We had a photographer come and take pictures and then my friend took video of the whole thing so there's an archive of it. I love that. Mom, you and Dad spawned more than half of the nearly one hundred in the family, though there were closer to eighty at the gathering. Starting with the next generation, by last count it was twenty-seven nieces and nephews, twenty-two great-nieces and great-nephews, ten great-great-nieces and great-great-nephews. It was so cool to see different versions of your face or Dad's face in so many of the young people. *Oh, God, he looks just like Mom when he laughs . . . Wow, she has the same gait that Kent does . . . That's the spitting image of Sheila . . . He's got the same complexion as Dad . . .* that sort of thing. And all of them, or anyway all but those who married into the family, carry on the tradition of being good, bad, and indifferent Andersons, and always interesting Andersons. (And maybe some of those who married in, too.)

I sometimes say I'm 20 percent Norwegian, 80 percent butter. That we're from the Land O'Lakes tribe.

But this is who I am, Mom. These are our people.

You'd be really proud. Several of the kids are in college. One of your descendants is starting medical school. And so many others have turned out to be quite something. The sky's the limit. Every generation seems to get healthier and better, and gatherings like these are really important so that we can all know each other, connect with each other, love each other.

It was truly a wonderful day. Like I said, it rained for most of it but the skies cleared later and Jimmy renewed his vows with his sweetheart, Lela, whom he met in his seventies. Can you believe it, Mom? I was the best man. Jimmy's son David married them—he got ordained just so he could do that. A really lovely exclamation point to a lovely event, and I'm so glad to see Jimmy so happy and Lela so happy and she's been so good to the boys.

You would be thrilled by it all, Mom—"proud as punch," as Minnesota icon Hubert Humphrey used to say.

And, Mom: one of the babies in the family is named Ora Zella!

You did it! You're still alive! So there's a baby with your name, and a son who plays you every Tuesday night on FX.

Mom, are you having a partial family reunion? Tell everyone we miss them and I hope that Dad has straightened out, and everybody is happy and loving and caring up there.

I want to believe there are lots of good things to come. There was lots of hugging and kissing at our reunion, Mom.

Lots of love,

Louie, just one of many descendants of Ora Zella Anderson

Season 3

Hey Mom,

The cast and director and writers all did a table read of Season 3 of *Baskets* at Zach's house. It was a wonderful experience. We had pizza brought in for the gang. Me, I had lots of salad.

A year ago it would have bothered me to not have any pizza. I would have been thinking about it the whole time we were reading each of the ten scripts. But it's okay now. Writing all these letters to you has made me realize something: Life is finite. (Duh.) Time is valuable. (Ditto.) And so am I. I'm valuable. I'm starting to treat myself as if I'm valuable. I don't get the potato chips. I go right for the celery, the carrot, the cucumber, the cauliflower—our favorite vegetable, Mom. Who doesn't love cauliflower? I'm in a different frame. I love vegetables once I get going with them. I don't graze. I don't get the sloppy joe. I don't get the doughnut—Mom, I've lost count of how many hundreds, maybe thousands, of doughnuts I've passed up from the *Baskets* Craft Services setup. (Though, for historical purposes, let me tell you that they had Cronuts the other day, and I know you would love a Cronut, a flaky doughnut that didn't exist when you were alive but, thanks to breakthroughs in pastry research, brought together the croissant and the doughnut.)

I am figuring out a way to heal, to "work the steps," as we say in the program. I reach out to others for help when I need it.

I'm back in Los Angeles for the next three months. I heard from the producer that they've made me a wig for Season 3 that cost nine thousand dollars. Can you believe it? *Nine thousand dollars!* (And it's not like we're a big-budget show.) Why so expensive? They hand-tie every single hair individually to a mesh shell that has thousands of tiny holes. Supposedly it will look more like my hair than my hair does. I can't wait to see it. Christine is moving up in the world.

I found this little apartment over in Studio City, in the Valley, because I know we're going to be doing a lot of shooting in the Valley. You remember Studio City, Mom? I'm pretty sure you were there with me once. I should have taken you to a lot more places. I should have done a lot more nice things for you. I'm so sorry that I wasn't a better son. But I'm trying not to play that song over and over.

Love,

Louie

The Sorrow Sparrow

Hey Mom,

Am I a sorrow sponge?

I leave myself wide open. I was heading out of town for a gig in Chicago and I saw a young woman at my airport gate who weighed well over three hundred pounds. She was short, too. And all I wanted to do was wrap my arms around her, just wanted to hold her because I knew how much pain she was probably in.

She was in her twenties, a young woman with beautiful purple braids. I told her I loved her hair. The flight was delayed. In the old days, a flight delay would have made me all *Damn this!* and *Screw that!* Instead, we talked. Mia was her name. She seemed nervous about flying. She was in phone sales. At one point I went to the newsstand to buy some bottled water and see if they had anything healthy to snack on, and I asked Mia if I could get her something, not too pushy, though, and she shook her head sweetly, sadly, Thank you, no. While I was at the newsstand I looked back and saw that she was drinking some sugary-type drink, and sneaking a bite of an Almond Joy while scrolling through her phone, and I imagined myself returning from my errand and going right up to her and reading her the Riot Act and asking her if she would go to my 12-step meeting with me—but when I returned I said nothing. I gave her a hug as we boarded the plane. After we landed at

O'Hare, I saw her again. "There you are," I said. "You made it." I thought of asking her if we could take a picture. "Mia, I've always loved that name. You know why? Because I'm always thinking of mee-a." It made her laugh. I thought about asking her to exchange emails, thinking maybe I could be helpful to her, but it seemed too forward. I should have.

This is my new life. Maybe I've always been this way but now I'm trying to be more proactive about it. Ours is the burden of food and for all my struggles, I thought I could maybe help her find her way out. She was probably suffering beyond belief. And no one really knows what to do about it. It moved me, to meet and talk with Mia. I don't think I'm seeing these people by chance. I don't know what anyone or anything is telling me—full moons or fat hummingbirds or colors swirling in the bathroom light, or you, Mom, now almost literally guiding me every time I dress up as Christine . . . but I feel there's some reason for all this.

Anyway, Mom, you would do the same—compliment someone on her hair, what a nice dress she was wearing, what a pretty smile she had, and then just make friends with her. Were you just getting to know them, Mom, or did you see something in them that you needed? Or see something in yourself that you thought they needed? Regardless, it's who we are, Mom. We can't control it. We're suckers for people. There's nothing we can do about it. We're people pleasers. There isn't anything else, really. That's why everyone watches TV and movies: whether the story is real or make-believe, we're interested in seeing what happens to people. Because we're all trying to figure ourselves out.

What a cruel world we live in—that someone has to be three hundred or four hundred pounds. That's the drug of this generation. I always see the bigger people in a way that many others don't.

Some people don't have easy lives. They just don't.

I think a lot of women are sad.

Men, too, of course. But I see the sad women out there, mostly because I'm playing Christine.

I watched Mia walk away, in the direction of baggage claim, walk slowly but still more spryly than I walk now, because she still has youth on her side. The sorrow sparrow landed on my shoulder.

Here's my goal with Christine: A lot of people know a Christine. A lot of people *are* Christine. Mom, let me share an email a viewer sent me this morning.

> Good morning, Mr. Anderson. I'm writing to thank you for all you do, you've always made me laugh. I really needed it. When I was going through a hard time, your character on baskets (AKA christine) lifted my spirits, somehow you channeled my mom, which really made me happy, because she's not with me anymore, which I needed.

I loved that "AKA."

I get stuff like this every day—posts on Facebook, tweets, messages on Instagram, emails. Some of it is devastating. Some of it is inspiring. Often I can't separate the two.

I really want to help people, Mom. I want to be nicer to everybody, not just when they have sorrow (though sorrow is always lurking, always). That's what you were all about, being kind all the time, no matter what. There's a chain reaction to being kind. People showed up at your funeral that none of us knew about, or they said they'd met you only once. They just wanted to be there. For you. For themselves.

A few years ago, when I went on the TV show *Splash* and faced my fear of heights, I think it gave some others strength. Not *think*, I *know*. Because lots of people came up to me in the months after my episode aired and told me things like, "I learned to swim because of you," "I started to swim again because of you," and "I started to face some of my fears, thank you so much, Louie."

I try my best always to put myself in everyone's position, Mom. At the hotel, the room service gentleman lugs a cart full of orders, doing his best to get everyone's right. This one wants to have his coffee with this kind of cream, that one says can you make sure I get a spoon I like, is there a fork in there, can you make sure the food comes up hot, can you make sure the ice isn't melted, you call this an entrée, this is really all the damn shrimp in the shrimp cocktail . . . Suppose I'm the twelfth person he's dealt with today, Mom. Has he had an easy time of it? Are those carts easy to move around? How can they be, with hotel carpet that thick? He just wants to get in and out of each room and each encounter, do his job right, and move on to the next. You can't blame room service people. They enter each room like they've been jumped or attacked before. So I put myself in his place. I say, "How is your day going? Are you busy down there? If anyone is giving you a bad time, tell me, I'll go down and talk to them about it." Why not put myself in the position of empathizing and understanding, since I so easily *could* be in that position? It could be me who's delivering the food and, frankly, wants to eat some of it on the way up. Does the guest in Room 1405 really know he's supposed to get four little muffins with his breakfast, not three?

The maid comes in to make up the bed and I actually want to make my own bed, because since I started with the 12-step program I've been making my own bed, decided to stop asking people to wait on me and start taking care of myself because if I don't, then I'll have lower expectations of myself. So I ask the maid, "How's your morning going?" She's taken aback. She smiles. We talk. She has a daughter applying to law school. I tell the maid I don't need anything, not even the bed made. "No, not even?" she says. She looks alarmed. I assure her it's okay. She asks if she can punch her code into my room phone to show her boss she's been to the room. "Punch away!" I say, almost giddy. "Get that code in there!" I asked her for the code so I could punch it in every day, so she could just skip my room. She just smiled.

You aren't what you eat. You aren't what you say. You are what you do.

I feel like right now I'm the best Louie I can be. I can get even better.

Good night, Mom. I don't feel sorrow right now.

Love,

Louie

Defending Champ

Hey Mom,

In my heart, I think I can win it again.

Everyone already has Alec Baldwin winning this year's Emmy for Outstanding Supporting Actor in a Comedy Series. And the Donald Trump impersonation he does on *Saturday Night Live* is great, really. (Remember what you used to say about Donald Trump, Mom? He's president of the United States now.) Alec gets the "watercooler" buzz because his appearances are commentaries on what happened in politics that week, even within the previous day or two. Since Hollywood is not very happy with Donald Trump, the Emmy voters might want to say something with their choice. We'll see. Every Academy voter is supposed to watch one episode of each of the nominees—in my category that's Baldwin, Tituss Burgess (again) on *Unbreakable Kimmy Schmidt*, Ty Burrell (again) on *Modern Family*, Tony Hale and Matt Walsh (again, again) on *Veep*, and me. All of them are truly outstanding (that sounds like I'm already giving my acceptance speech). We submitted the "Denver" episode to show my work as Christine. I think it's a great episode, some really beautiful work with Alex Morris as Ken. After discussing with her mother the idea of meeting someone to date, Christine decides to take a chance and overcome her fear of rejection so she doesn't end up alone, and can live a little, maybe even twirl a little.

Even if I don't win, I'm content with what I'm doing. I know I'm just playing who this woman is.

And I have to reflect on how glad I am just to be working.

Ahmos, my manager, will accompany me this afternoon to the Emmys. You only get two tickets. I wish I could take you, Mom. If you were here, you'd sit next to me and we'd have to buy a third ticket for Ahmos, for seven hundred dollars. I'll probably also sit near Zach, who was nominated this year for Outstanding Lead Actor, which he deserved. He really deserved two nominations, since he plays Dale Baskets *and* Chip Baskets. I told him last year he would get nominated this time. He often plays a funny person but there's such depth to his characters and such breadth to his talent. He never telegraphs what he's going to do. His unbelievable work in Season 2 made me work harder and strive to do more. Oh, and Jonathan got nominated for director, which he so deeply deserved.

Anyway, Mom, wish me luck—again . . .

Love,

Louie

The Day You Died

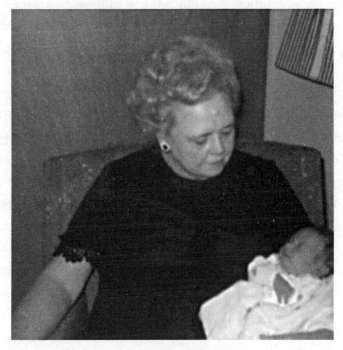

Mom and grandchild

Hey Mom,

It's the letter I've been thinking about and dreading since I started writing you letters a couple years ago. Maybe you've been dreading it, too, mostly because you feel my pain. This is the worst, hardest letter I will write. But we often have to do the things we hate, right? So I need to do this.

I thought you were going to live forever.

The day a mom dies is the day her child's life changes forever. It's the first time you really, truly feel mortality, because the person who brought you into this world is no longer there. You are forced to confront the idea that you might actually be mortal because up until then you were invincible. You were so very powerful because the person who brought you into the world was there, there with you, and you were both alive, and in your existence you had both always been alive.

But then she dies.

And something in you dies. *So I guess that means . . . I could die*, you think. When she dies, part of your heart stops beating. Something loosens in you, something that gave you stability and comfort. And now you're no longer as secure on the stage of life. Now you realize that things could come crashing down around you. When the person who brought you into the world, who wiped your chin and wiped your butt, who was there for you and protected you and shaped you, who gave you an identity when you didn't have one . . . when you lose that lifeline, it's like the movie *Gravity*, and now you're floating in space and hoping to hell that someone will catch you or you can grab a line that you can tether yourself to. It's the very first day you feel that maybe you could die.

January 4, 1990, I was in Minneapolis. I had performed on New Year's Eve and decided to stay over a few days, down at the old flour mill that became a hotel. Which meant the rooms were a little smaller, the hallways a little darker, the windows a little weirder than a hotel built as a hotel. But I was comfortable in my room and fell asleep early.

I woke to a ringing telephone. Ringing and ringing and ringing and ringing and ringing. I didn't know if it was a real phone ringing or a dream of a phone ringing. I did not know where I was. You know I sleep on my side, Mom, and the phone was behind me, and I did not want to turn over and face whatever it was, whoever it was, whatever reason it was ringing and ringing. Yet even as I tried to ignore it, I was becoming more and more awake, and I looked toward the door and there you were.

Only it was a much bigger version of you, practically a giant figure of you, with what seemed like thousands of beams of light coming out of you, with a thousand scarves flowing and blowing around the room, but scarves that are completely transparent, more like wisps of light than a solid material. Some of the colors I had never seen before, so I can't even describe them. It made me smile and feel love. I reached my hand toward some of the scarves and colors that were nearest but it felt as if something was touching me, as if I was being reached out to, a way of communicating, but I didn't know what. I felt a tug, and it was the back-and-forth between whatever was going on between us, and then the horrible hotel phone ringing, the explosive awful clanging punctuated by brief silences.

I rolled over to face the phone and the ringing dimmed. I looked back toward the door and marveled even more at this beautiful vision before me, a you-had-to-be-there moment, a sight I have tried to describe here but I know my description does not suffice. Finally, I put the phone to my ear—and all the light, all the color, all hope rushed out, as if a vacuum from out in the hallway sucked everything inside my room underneath the door.

I was in the dark again.

"Louie? Louie?" A familiar voice. Anderson. Brother. Third.

"Yeah," I must have said, automatically.

"It's Jimmy. Mom died."

I don't know how long it was before I simply said, "Shit."

There was another pause, by me, for how long I don't know. Finally, with a sense of purpose, I said, "Hold on a minute, Jimmy."

I put down the phone, stood, walked to the door, opened it, and looked down the hallway. I was looking for that vision, that light, that love, that hope that had just been present in the room, now realizing that you had been saying a final earthly goodbye. There was no sign of you.

Yet the hallway was brighter than it had been before, I swear. You had left something behind. Maybe a message. A little hope. Assurance that you had been there, that you took time before you ascended to give me a last loving Ora Zella Anderson hug.

When I picked up the phone again, Jimmy told me the details. You were in your car and it had stalled. Mom, you used to snap your fingers and say, "When I die, I want to go like that." Well, you died in your car. Fortunately, the car wasn't moving when you had the massive heart attack. It was over as quick as a snap of your fingers.

It's a long life but not as long as I wished. Maybe every kid says that, no matter when their mom goes. You outlived Dad, Mom, by ten years. (He was also twelve years older than you, so your life spans were almost the same.)

When your mom dies, you realize that you, too, will one day die. It finally, really hits home. But in thinking about these really sad things, you eventually realize something else: You're here, thinking about these things. You're still here. So that must mean that when things come crashing down around you, you can still get up. You can rise from the ashes, climb out from the destruction. You can still make something happen, something good. It's possible. Just like I knew how much I did not want to write this letter, and hated the idea of writing this letter, here I am . . . writing this letter.

When Mom dies, you dread doing anything new, anything more, anything else. But you have to. You have to right the ship. You have to right things that are wrong, as best you can. You find strength you didn't know you had.

I guess I'm glad this letter is over.

Love,

Your thankful child, Louie

To Everyone Who Is
a Mom or Had a Mom

Hey Mom—and all other moms and dads,

So that's about all I have to say. I think I've said a lot. (Oh, yeah: I didn't win the second Emmy. Alec Baldwin, the betting favorite, nabbed it. That's politics for you!) (No, he was really very good.) (Really!)

I'm glad I took the time to talk to you and send all my feelings and love to you.

I have messages for all the other mothers and fathers out there:

Thank you just for being there. God bless you all.

That's the first message. Here's the second one:

Keep doing what you do best. Keep loving us. Keep looking after us.

But don't stop there. No.

Pick a day where all the mothers and fathers of the world, from end to end, every single one of you, at the same time, walk out the front door of your house, your hovel, your hacienda, your palace, your mud hut, your cottage, your apartment, your yurt, your trailer, your igloo, your houseboat, your room, your tent tethered to a fence on Skid Row—step outside. All of you.

Then, each of you, make sure that each of your sons and daughters is within earshot. Better yet, have them within arm's reach.

Now, take up the hand of each of your children, and all the mothers and fathers together say this:

"Let's change the world. Because it isn't working the way it is. Can we all start with a little more kindness, please?"

For the first thirty-six years of my life, I watched my mother's genius for kindness. Her talent for making family and friends feel close, and strangers just as close. Her ability to be charitable, tactful, loving, and non-judgmental. I have used these as guiding virtues for Christine Baskets.

Nothing is easy when it comes to people changing. But moms have a lot of power. Dads, too. You are the architects of love, our first teachers, preachers, and cheerleaders, the ones who have seen us at our best and our worst, who know us through and through. And *you* are going to save the world, moms and dads, by getting the ones you love and who love you to be a little different from those who came before.

Moms and dads have a special power, tremendous and in some ways not close to fully tapped. What if we said we were all going to do it for the moms and the dads?

Because it isn't working the way it is.

If saying things gently doesn't make an impact, parents, then try this:

"Hey, everybody, knock it off! Stop treating each other so badly! I expect more from you! I expect you, my son, my daughter, to stop and look around and realize that we are all connected. We are all alike. We are all living on this earth together. And we're not going back into the house for coffee and cake until you truly acknowledge that! We screwed up, screwed up terribly, but we're never going to stop expecting better from you. We're not going to accept less. Because if we do, then the world's over, it's the end of the world as we know it. For thousands of years, humankind has not gotten it right. So . . . get your act together! Be the first act that's really gotten it together! Love more and hate less. Do for others. Make the right decision, which you usually know what it is. Be the person you can really be because we know you have it in you and we can't go on like this! Wake up, smell the roses, do something for somebody, love somebody, care for somebody. Change direction. If you change your desires, you have to replace them with something, and it should be something that will be helpful to other people, to this world, to this earth, to this universe . . . I'm your mom/dad! Honor me as I honored *you*! If you can't do it for yourself, do it for me!"

Hey Mom: I want you to know that I'm taking better care of myself. I wish everyone would take better care of themselves. Christine is doing all she can to take better care of herself. Now we just need the world to do the same.

You were and still are the best mom ever. I'm finished with the book but I'll keep talking about you and to you forever.

Love & gratitude,

Louie, Ora's son

Acknowledgments

Many people were helpful to me in making this book. Thank you to my brothers, sisters, and considerable family, to Abraham Geisness, Ahmos Hassan, Yfat Reiss Gendell, Susan Moldow, Matthew Benjamin, Madeleine Morel, Eve and Glenn Schwartz, Nicole Favale, everyone at FX, and my *Baskets* family.

Most important, thank you to Andrew Postman, who made the impossible possible by helping a procrastinating kid from the Roosevelt Projects who hated homework and finishing things *do* that homework and finish this book, a tribute to my beautiful, deserving mother. Thanks, Andy!

Thank you all for helping me do more and be more—and say just enough!

Love,

Louie